THE PLAYS OF OSCAR WILDE
VOLUME I

THE PLAYS OF OSCAR WILDE
VOLUME I

Lady Windermere's Fan

and

A Woman of No Importance

WORDSWORTH CLASSICS

This edition published 1997
by Wordsworth Editions Limited
Cumberland House, Crib Street, Ware,
Hertfordshire SG12 9ET

ISBN 1 85326 184 X

*Printed and bound in Great Britain
by Mackays of Chatham plc, Chatham, Kent
Typeset in the UK by R & B Creative Services Limited*

INTRODUCTION

WHEN OSCAR WILDE decided to abandon serious tragedy and write comedy, he did so for financial reasons. He delivered the manuscript for *Lady Windermere's Fan*, to the manager of St. James' Theatre explaining it as 'one of those modern drawing-room plays with pink lampshades'. This was a formula that was to serve him well.

Lady Windermere's Fan opened on 20th February 1892 and was an overwhelming success. As the final curtain fell that night, the audience clamoured for the author to appear, which he did, still smoking a cigarette, and saying with characteristic audacity:

> 'Ladies and gentlemen, I have enjoyed this evening immensely. The actors have given us a charming rendition of a delightful play, and your appreciation has been most intelligent. I congratulate you on the great success of your performance which persuades me that you think almost as highly of the play as I do myself.'

The popularity of *Lady Windermere's Fan* rested principally on its dazzling dialogue, but it was also a well made play. It obeys Aristotelian unity of time, the action taking place within twenty-four hours, has a balanced cast, and an opening act which reveals themes that are developed within the course of the play. Its plot, like those of the next three plays Wilde was to write, revolves around a guilty secret. Mrs. Erlynne is a woman with a past. Initially presented as a blackmailer, her sudden jeopardizing of her own respectable future for the sake of her daughter's reputation defies all expectations, and causes a shift in dramatic sympathy that compels attention.

Wilde had originally called the play "The Good Woman", a title reflecting the play's insidious social criticism, but also containing a double-edged irony. Mrs. Erlynne may perform one selfless maternal act, but in every other respect she is grasping, ruthless, and hardly 'good'. Wilde's play attacks a society which is too prompt to condemn, but he also subtly exposes paradoxes of personality, and the way in which a manipulative woman can overcome scandal and turn events to her own advantage.

The most commanding male part in the play is that of Lord Darlington, a vehicle for Wilde's sharpest epigrams, who mocks pretention. 'Experience is the name men give to their mistakes', he remarks or 'Nowadays, to be intelligible is to be found out'. Minor characters create the social ambience with their glamour and frivolity, disclosing vital information as they gossip, and at the heart of the play, Lady Windermere's fan – lavish, decorative, unnecessary, – is a potent image of the values of the mercenary society depicted. Every character in the play is ultimately driven by self-interest alone, but Wilde's satire is softened by sympathy, humour and the beauty of his settings.

Wilde's next play, *A Woman of no Importance*, opened at the Haymarket Theatre on 19th April, 1893. Critics were not over impressed, attacking its deficiencies of plot, but Wilde refuted them with aplomb:

> 'Plots are tedious. Anyone can invent them. Life is full of them. Indeed one has to elbow one's way through them as they crowd across one's path. I took the plot of this play from *The Family Herald* which took it, wisely, I feel – from my novel *The Picture of Dorian Gray*. People love a wicked aristocrat who seduces a virtuous maiden, and they love virtuous maiden for being seduced by a wicked aristocrat. I have given them what they like, so that they may learn to appreciate what I like to give them.'

His arrogance was justified by his audiences who did indeed love the play. Again Wilde observed unity of time, and all the action takes place at or near Hunstanton Chase, the country seat of Lord Illingworth. Again a woman with a secret is at the centre of a 'drawing-room' drama which illuminates the moral ambivalences of a society whose intolerance is hypocritical. The slight action consists of many dramatic reversals, mostly wrought by Hester Worsley, the young American heiress who counterpoints the attitudes and Wildean epigrams of Lord Illingworth with her feminist diatribes and puritanical attitudes. As a foreigner she is not bound by the prevailing social code and is a useful device for open criticism. The sexual exploitation of women is the main theme of the play, but Mrs. Arbuthnot, Wilde's exploited heroine, is shown to be a surprisingly strong woman with revolutionary ideas for the time. Like Ibsen's heroines, she refuses to conform to the proprieties of conventional morality. Her motivation is very different, but like Mrs. Erlynne in *Lady Windermere's Fan* and indeed the women of Wilde's later comedies, she knows and gets what she wants, while the men in these plays are so often 'of no importance'. The title of this play, too, carries its own irony.

Oscar Wilde's wit is legendary, and the hilarity that it provides implies a forgiveness of his characters that is winning. Writing in the tradition of distinguished Irish comic dramatists such as Congreve, Sheridan and Goldsmith, Wilde takes simple, even absurd plots from Victorian melodrama and farce and raises them to a plane of high sophistication with his brilliantly polished dialogue. His attacks on society retain a delicacy of touch that may cause his serious intention to be overlooked, but provides extremely effective and entertaining theatre.

Further reading:

Oscar Wilde, *The Picture of Dorian Gray*, Wordsworth Editions, London, 1992.

Oscar Wilde, *Lord Arthur Saville's Crime*, Wordsworth Editions, London, 1993.

Richard Ellman, *Oscar Wilde*, London, 1987.

Melissa Knox, *Oscar Wilde, A Long and Lovely Suicide*, New Haven and London, 1957.

A. Bird, *The Plays of Oscar Wilde*, London, 1977.

E. R. Bentley, *The Playwright as a Thinker*, London, 1946.

Lord Alfred Douglas, *The Autobiography of Lord Alfred Douglas*, London 1929.

Robert Hitchens, *The Green Carnation*, London, 1894.

Vyvyan Holland, *Son of Oscar Wilde*, London and Tonbridge, 1954.

Contents

———————◆———————

PREFACE

The artist is the creator of beautiful things.

To reveal art and conceal the artist is art's aim.

The critic is he who can translate into another manner or a new material his impression of beautiful things.

The highest, as the lowest, form of criticism is a mode of autobiography.

Those who find ugly meanings in beautiful things are corrupt without being charming. This is a fault.

Those who find beautiful meanings in beautiful things are the cultivated. For these there is hope.

They are the elect to whom beautiful things mean only Beauty.

There is no such thing as a moral or an immoral book. Books are well written, or badly written. That is all.

The nineteenth century dislike of Realism is the rage of Caliban seeing his own face in a glass.

The nineteenth century dislike of Romanticism is the rage of Caliban not seeing his own face in a glass.

The moral life of man forms part of the subject matter of the artist, but the morality of art consists in the perfect use of an imperfect medium. No artist desires to prove anything. Even things that are true can be proved.

No artist has ethical sympathies. An ethical sympathy in an artist is an unpardonable mannerism of style.

No artist is ever morbid. The artist can express everything.

Thought and language are to the artist instruments of an art.

Vice and virtue are to the artist materials for an art.

From the point of view of form, the type of all the arts is the art of the musician. From the point of view of feeling, the actor's craft is the type.

All art is at once surface and symbol.

Those who go beneath the surface do so at their peril.

Those who read the symbol do so at their peril.

It is the spectator, and not life, that art really mirrors. Diversity of opinion about a work of art shows that the work is new, complex, and vital.

When critics disagree the artist is in accord with himself.

We can forgive a man for making a useful thing as long as he does not admire it. The only excuse for making a useless thing is that one admires it intensely. All art is quite useless.

OSCAR WILDE.

LADY WINDERMERE'S FAN

TO
THE DEAR MEMORY
OF
ROBERT EARL OF LYTTON
IN AFFECTION
AND
ADMIRATION

THE PERSONS OF THE PLAY

LORD WINDERMERE
LORD DARLINGTON
LORD AUGUSTUS LORTON
MR. DUMBY
MR. CECIL GRAHAM
MR. HOPPER
PARKER, Butler

LADY WINDERMERE
THE DUCHESS OF BERWICK
LADY AGATHA CARLISLE
LADY PLYMDALE
LADY STUTFIELD
LADY JEDBURGH
MRS. COWPER-COWPER
MRS. ERLYNNE
ROSALIE, Maid

THE SCENES OF THE PLAY

ACT I. *Morning-room in Lord Windermere's house.*
ACT II. *Drawing-room in Lord Windermere's house.*
ACT III. *Lord Darlington's rooms.*
ACT IV. *Same as Act I.*

TIME: *The Present.*
PLACE: *London.*

The action of the play takes place within twenty-four hours, beginning on a Tuesday afternoon at five o'clock, and ending the next day at 1.30 p.m.

LONDON ST. JAMES'S THEATRE

Lessee and Manager: Mr. George Alexander
February 22nd, 1892

LORD WINDERMERE *Mr. George Alexander*
LORD DARLINGTON *Mr. Nutcombe Gould*
LORD AUGUSTUS LORTON   *Mr. H. H. Vincent*
MR. CECIL GRAHAM   *Mr. Ben Webster*
MR. DUMBY   *Mr. Vane-Tempest*
MR HOPPER   *Mr. Alfred Holles*
PARKER (Butler)   *Mr. V. Sansbury*
LADY WINDERMERE *Miss Lily Hanbury*
THE DUCHESS OF BERWICK *Miss Fanny Coleman*
LADY AGATHA CARLISLE   *Miss Laura Graves*
LADY PLYMDALE   *Miss Granville*
LADY JEDBURGH   *Miss B. Page*
LADY STUTFIELD   *Miss Madge Girdlestone*
MRS. COWPER-COWPER   *Miss A. de Winton*
MRS. ERLYNNE   *Miss Marion Terry*
ROSALIE (Maid)   *Miss Winifred Dolan*

FIRST ACT

SCENE

Morning-room of Lord Windermere's house in Carlton House Terrace. Doors C. and R. Bureau with books and papers R. Sofa with small tea-table L. Window opening on to terrace L. Table R.

LADY WINDERMERE *is at table R., arranging roses in a blue bowl.*

Enter PARKER.

Parker: Is your ladyship at home this afternoon?

Lady Windermere: Yes – who has called?

Parker: Lord Darlington, my lady.

Lady Windermere (hesitates for a moment): Show him up – and I'm at home to any one who calls.

Parker: Yes, my lady. (*Exit C.*)

Lady Windermere: It's best for me to see him before to-night. I'm glad he's come.

Enter PARKER *C.*

Parker: Lord Darlington.

Enter LORD DARLINGTON *C.*
Exit PARKER.

Lord Darlington: How do you do, Lady Windermere?

Lady Windermere: How do you do, Lord Darlington? No, I can't shake hands with you. My hands are all wet with these roses. Aren't they lovely? They came up from Selby this morning.

Lord Darlington: They are quite perfect. (*Sees a fan lying on the table.*) And what a wonderful fan! May I look at it?

Lady Windermere: Do. Pretty, isn't it! It's got my name on it, and everything. I have only just seen it myself. It's my husband's birthday present to me. You know to-day is my birthday?

Lord Darlington: No? Is it really?

Lady Windermere: Yes, I'm of age to-day. Quite an important day in my life, isn't it? That is why I am giving this party to-night. Do sit down. (*Still arranging flowers.*)

Lord Darlington (*sitting down*): I wish I had known it was your birthday, Lady Windermere. I would have covered the whole street in front of your house with flowers for you to walk on. They are made for you. (*A short pause.*)

Lady Windermere: Lord Darlington, you annoyed me last night at the Foreign Office. I am afraid you are going to annoy me again.

Lord Darlington: I, Lady Windermere?

Enter PARKER *and* FOOTMAN *C., with tray and tea things.*

Lady Windermere: Put it there, Parker. That will do. (*Wipes her hands with her pocket-handkerchief, goes to tea-table L., and sits down.*) Won't you come over, Lord Darlington?

Exit PARKER *C.*

Lord Darlington (*takes chair and goes across L.C.*): I am quite miserable, Lady Windermere. You must tell me what I did. (*Sits down at table L.*)

Lady Windermere: Well, you kept paying me elaborate compliments the whole evening.

Lord Darlington (*smiling*): Ah, nowadays we are all of us so hard up, that the only pleasant things to pay are compliments. They're the only things we can pay.

Lady Windermere (*shaking her head*): No, I am talking very seriously. You mustn't laugh, I am quite serious. I don't like compliments, and I don't see why a man should think he is pleasing a woman enormously when he says to her a whole heap of things that he doesn't mean.

Lord Darlington: Ah, but I did mean them. (*Takes tea which she offers him.*)

Lady Windermere (*gravely*): I hope not. I should be sorry to have to quarrel with you, Lord Darlington. I like you very much, you know that. But I shouldn't like you at all if I thought you were what most other men are. Believe me, you are better than most other men, and I sometimes think you pretend to be worse.

Lord Darlington: We all have our little vanities, Lady Windermere.

Lady Windermere: Why do you make that your special one? (*Still seated at table L.*)

Lord Darlington (still seated L.C.): Oh, nowadays so many conceited people go about Society pretending to be good, that I think it shows rather a sweet and modest disposition to pretend to be bad. Besides, there is this to be said. If you pretend to be good, the world takes you very seriously. If you pretend to be bad, it doesn't. Such is the astounding stupidity of optimism.

Lady Windermere: Don't you want the world to take you seriously then, Lord Darlington?

Lord Darlington: No, not the world. Who are the people the world takes seriously? All the dull people one can think of, from the Bishops down to the bores. I should like *you* to take me very seriously, Lady Windermere, *you* more than any one else in life.

Lady Windermere: Why – why me?

Lord Darlington (after a slight hesitation): Because I think we might be great friends. Let us be great friends. You may want a friend some day.

Lady Windermere: Why do you say that?

Lord Darlington: Oh! – we all want friends at times.

Lady Windermere: I think we're very good friends already, Lord Darlington. We can always remain so as long as you don't –

Lord Darlington: Don't what?

Lady Windermere: Don't spoil it by saying extravagant silly things to me. You think I am a Puritan, I suppose? Well, I have something of the Puritan in me. I was brought up like that. I am glad of it. My mother died when I was a mere child. I lived always with Lady Julia, my father's elder sister, you know. She was stern to me, but she taught me what the world is forgetting, the difference that there is between what is right and what is wrong. She allowed of no compromise. I allow of none.

Lord Darlington: My dear Lady Windermere!

Lady Windermere (leaning back on the sofa): You look on me as being behind the age. – Well, I am! I should be sorry to be on the same level as an age like this.

Lord Darlington: You think the age very bad?

Lady Windermere: Yes. Nowadays people seem to look on life as a speculation. It is not a speculation. It is a sacrament. Its ideal is Love. Its purification is sacrifice.

Lord Darlington (smiling): Oh, anything is better than being sacrificed!

Lady Windermere (leaning forward): Don't say that.

Lord Darlington: I do say it. I felt it – I know it.

Enter PARKER *C.*

Parker: The men want to know if they are to put the carpets on the terrace for to-night my lady?

Lady Windermere: You don't think it will rain, Lord Darlington, do you?

Lord Darlington: I won't hear of its raining on your birthday.

Lady Windermere: Tell them to do it at once, Parker.

Exit PARKER *C.*

Lord Darlington (still seated): Do you think then – of course I am only putting an imaginary instance – do you think that in the case of a young married couple, say about two years married, if the husband suddenly becomes the intimate friend of a woman of – well, more than doubtful character – is always calling upon her, lunching with her, and probably paying her bills – do you think that the wife should not console herself?

Lady Windermere (frowning): Console herself?

Lord Darlington: Yes, I think she should – I think she has the right.

Lady Windermere: Because the husband is vile – should the wife be vile also?

Lord Darlington: Vileness is a terrible word, Lady Windermere.

Lady Windermere: It is a terrible thing, Lord Darlington.

Lord Darlington: Do you know I am afraid that good people do a great deal of harm in this world. Certainly the greatest harm they do is that they make badness of such extraordinary importance. It is absurd to divide people into good and bad. People are either charming or tedious. I take the side of the charming, and you, Lady Windermere, can't help belonging to them.

Lady Windermere: Now, Lord Darlington. (*Rising and crossing R., front of him.*) Don't stir, I am merely going to finish my flowers. (*Goes to table R.C.*)

Lord Darlington (rising and moving chair): And I must say I think you are very hard on modern life, Lady Windermere. Of course there is much against it, I admit. Most women, for instance, nowadays, are rather mercenary.

Lady Windermere: Don't talk about such people.

Lord Darlington: Well then, setting mercenary people aside, who, of course, are dreadful, do you think seriously that women who have committed what the world calls a fault should never be forgiven?

Lady Windermere (standing at table): I think they should never be forgiven.

Lord Darlington: And men? Do you think that there should be the same laws for men as there are for women?

Lady Windermere: Certainly!

Lord Darlington: I think life too complex a thing to be settled by these hard and fast rules.

Lady Windermere: If we had 'these hard and fast rules,' we should find life much more simple.

Lord Darlington: You allow of no exceptions?

Lady Windermere: None!

Lord Darlington: Ah, what a fascinating Puritan you are, Lady Windermere!

Lady Windermere: The adjective was unnecessary, Lord Darlington.

Lord Darlington: I couldn't help it. I can resist everything except temptation.

Lady Windermere: You have the modern affectation of weakness.

Lord Darlington (looking at her): It's only an affectation, Lady Windermere.

Enter PARKER *C.*

Parker: The Duchess of Berwick and Lady Agatha Carlisle.

Enter the DUCHESS OF BERWICK *and* LADY AGATHA CARLISLE *C.*

Exit PARKER *C.*

Duchess of Berwick (coming down C. and shaking hands): Dear Margaret, I am so pleased to see you. You remember Agatha, don't you? *(Crossing L.C.)* How do you do, Lord Darlington? I won't let you know my daughter, you are far too wicked.

Lord Darlington: Don't say that, Duchess. As a wicked man I am a complete failure. Why, there are lots of people who say I have never really done anything wrong in the whole course of my life. Of course they only say it behind my back.

Duchess of Berwick: Isn't he dreadful? Agatha, this is Lord Darlington. Mind you don't believe a word he says. (LORD DARLINGTON *crosses R.C.*) No, no tea, thank you, dear. *(Crosses and sits on sofa.)* We have just had tea at Lady Markby's. Such bad tea, too. It was quite undrinkable. I wasn't at all surprised. Her own son-in-law supplies it. Agatha is looking forward so much to your ball to-night, dear Margaret.

Lady Windermere (seated L.C.): Oh, you mustn't think it is going to be a ball, Duchess. It is only a dance in honour of my birthday. A small and early.

Lord Darlington (standing L.C.): Very small, very early, and very select, Duchess.

Duchess of Berwick (on sofa L.): Of course it's going to be select. But we know *that*, dear Margaret, about *your* house. It is really one of the few houses in London where I can take Agatha, and where I feel perfectly secure about dear Berwick. I don't know what society is coming to. The most dreadful people seem to go everywhere. They certainly come to my parties – the men get quite furious if one doesn't ask them. Really, some one should make a stand against it.

Lady Windermere: I will, Duchess. I will have no one in my house about whom there is any scandal.

Lord Darlington (R.C.): Oh, don't say that, Lady Windermere. I should never be admitted! (*Sitting.*)

Duchess of Berwick: Oh, men don't matter. With women it is different. We're good. Some of us are, at least. But we are positively getting elbowed into the corner. Our husbands would really forget our existence if we didn't nag at them from time to time, just to remind them that we have a perfect legal right to do so.

Lord Darlington: It's a curious thing, Duchess, about the game of marriage – a game, by the way, that is going out of fashion – the wives hold all the honours, and invariably lose the odd trick.

Duchess of Berwick: The odd trick? Is that the husband, Lord Darlington?

Lord Darlington: It would be rather a good name for the modern husband.

Duchess of Berwick: Dear Lord Darlington, how thoroughly depraved you are!

Lady Windermere: Lord Darlington is trivial.

Lord Darlington: Ah, don't say that, Lady Windermere.

Lady Windermere: Why do you *talk* so trivially about life, then?

Lord Darlington: Because I think that life is far too important a thing ever to talk seriously about it. (*Moves up C.*)

Duchess of Berwick: What does he mean? Do, as a concession to my poor wits, Lord Darlington, just explain to me what you really mean.

Lord Darlington (coming down back of table): I think I had better not, Duchess. Nowadays to be intelligible is to be found out. Good-bye! (*Shakes hands with* DUCHESS.) And now – (*goes up stage*) – Lady Windermere, good-bye. I may come to-night, mayn't I? Do let me come.

Lady Windermere (*standing up stage with* LORD DARLING-TON): Yes, certainly. But you are not to say foolish, insincere things to people.

Lord Darlington (*smiling*): Ah! you are beginning to reform me. It is a dangerous thing to reform any one, Lady Windermere. (*Bows, and exit C.*)

Duchess of Berwick (*who has risen, goes C.*): What a charming, wicked creature! I like him so much. I'm quite delighted he's gone! How sweet you're looking! Where *do* you get your gowns? And now I must tell you how sorry I am for you, dear Margaret. (*Crosses to sofa and sits with* LADY WINDERMERE.) Agatha, darling!

Lady Agatha: Yes, mamma. (*Rises.*)

Duchess of Berwick: Will you go and look over the photograph album that I see there?

Lady Agatha: Yes, mamma. (*Goes to table up L.*)

Duchess of Berwick: Dear girl! She is so fond of photographs of Switzerland. Such a pure taste, I think. But I really am so sorry for you, Margaret.

Lady Windermere (*smiling*): Why, Duchess?

Duchess of Berwick: Oh, on account of that horrid woman. She dresses so well, too, which makes it much worse, sets such a dreadful example. Augustus – you know my disreputable brother – such a trial to us all – well, Augustus is completely infatuated about her. It is quite scandalous, for she is absolutely inadmissible into society. Many a woman has a past, but I am told that she has at least a dozen, and that they all fit.

Lady Windermere: Whom are you talking about, Duchess?

Duchess of Berwick: About Mrs. Erlynne.

Lady Windermere: Mrs. Erlynne? I never heard of her, Duchess. And what *has* she to do with me?

Duchess of Berwick: My poor child! Agatha, darling!

Lady Agatha: Yes, mamma.

Duchess of Berwick: Will you go out on the terrace and look at the sunset?

Lady Agatha: Yes, mamma. (*Exit through window L.*)

Duchess of Berwick: Sweet girl! So devoted to sunsets! Shows such refinement of feeling, does it not? After all, there is nothing like Nature, is there?

Lady Windermere: But what is it, Duchess? Why do you talk to me about this person?

Duchess of Berwick: Don't you really know? I assure you we're all so distressed about it. Only last night at dear Lady Jansen's every one was saying how extraordinary it was that, of all men in London, Windermere should behave in such a way.

Lady Windermere: My husband – what has *he* got to do with any woman of that kind?

Duchess of Berwick: Ah, what indeed, dear? That is the point. He goes to see her continually, and stops for hours at a time, and while he is there she is not at home to any one. Not that many ladies call on her dear, but she has a great many disreputable men friends – my own brother particularly, as I told you – and that is what makes it so dreadful about Windermere. We looked upon *him* as being such a model husband, but I am afraid there is no doubt about it. My dear nieces – you know the Saville girls, don't you? – such nice domestic creatures – plain, dreadfully plain, but so good – well, they're always at the window doing fancy work, and making ugly things for the poor, which I think so useful of them in these dreadful socialistic days, and this terrible woman has taken a house in Curzon Street, right opposite them – such a respectable street, too! I don't know what we're coming to! And they tell me that Windermere goes there four and five times a week – they *see* him. They can't help it – and although they never talk scandal, they – well, of course – they remark on it to every one. And the worst of it all is that I have been told that this woman has got a great deal of money out of somebody, for it seems that she came to London six months ago without anything at all to speak of, and now she has this charming house in Mayfair, drives her ponies in the Park every afternoon and all – well, all – since she has known poor dear Windermere.

Lady Windermere: Oh, I can't believe it!

Duchess of Berwick: But it's quite true, my dear. The whole of London knows it. That is why I felt it was better to come and talk to you, and advise you to take Windermere away at once to Homburg or to Aix, where he'll have something to amuse him, and where you can watch him all day long. I assure you, my dear, that on several occasions after I was first married, I had to pretend to be very ill, and was obliged to drink the most unpleasant mineral waters, merely to get Berwick out of town. He was so extremely susceptible. Though I am bound to say he never gave away any large sums of money to anybody. He is far too high-principled for that!

Lady Windermere (*interrupting*): Duchess, Duchess, it's impossible! (*Rising and crossing stage to C.*): We are only married two years. Our child is but six months old. (*Sits in chair R. of L. table.*)

Duchess of Berwick: Ah, the dear pretty baby! How is the little darling? Is it a boy or a girl? I hope a girl – ah, no, I remember it's a boy! I'm so sorry. Boys are so wicked. My boy is excessively immoral. You wouldn't believe at what hours he comes home. And he's only left Oxford a few months – I really don't know what they teach them there.

Lady Windermere: Are *all* men bad?

Duchess of Berwick: Oh, all of them, my dear, all of them, without any exception, and they never grow any better. Men become old, but they never become good.

Lady Windermere: Windermere and I married for love.

Duchess of Berwick: Yes, we begin like that. It was only Berwick's brutal and incessant threats of suicide that made me accept him at all, and before the year was out, he was running after all kinds of petticoats, every colour, every shape, every material. In fact, before the honeymoon was over, I caught him winking at my maid, a most pretty, respectable girl. I dismissed her at once without a character. – No, I remember I passed her on to my sister; poor dear Sir George is so short-sighted, I thought it wouldn't matter. But it did, though – it was most unfortunate. (*Rises.*) And now, my dear child, I must go, as we are dining out. And mind you don't take this little aberration of Windermere's too much to heart. Just take him abroad, and he'll come back to you all right.

Lady Windermere: Come back to me? (*C.*)

Duchess of Berwick (*L.C.*): Yes, dear, these wicked women get our husbands away from us, but they always come back, slightly damaged, of course. And don't make scenes, men hate them!

Lady Windermere: It is very kind of you, Duchess, to come and tell all this. But I can't believe that my husband is untrue to me.

Duchess of Berwick: Pretty child! I was like that once. Now I know that all men are monsters. (LADY WINDERMERE *rings bell.*) The only thing to do is to feed the wretches well. A good cook does wonders, and that I know you have. My dear Margaret, you are not going to cry?

Lady Windermere: You needn't be afraid, Duchess, I never cry.

Duchess of Berwick: That's quite right, dear. Crying is the refuge of plain women but the ruin of pretty ones. Agatha, darling!

Lady Agatha (*entering L.*): Yes, mamma. (*Stands back of table L.C.*)

Duchess of Berwick: Come and bid good-bye to Lady Windermere, and thank her for your charming visit. (*Coming down again*): And by the way, I must thank you for sending a card to Mr. Hopper – he's that rich young Australian people are taking such notice of just at present. His father made a great fortune by selling some kind of food in circular tins – most palatable, I believe – I fancy it is the thing the servants always refuse to eat. But the son is quite interesting. I think he's attracted by dear Agatha's clever talk. Of course, we should be very sorry to lose her, but I think that a mother who doesn't part with a daughter every season has no real affection. We're coming to-night, dear. (PARKER *opens C. doors.*) And remember my advice, take the poor fellow out of town at once, it is the only thing to do. Goodbye, once more; come, Agatha.

Exeunt DUCHESS *and* LADY AGATHA *C.*

Lady Windermere: How horrible! I understand now what Lord Darlington meant by the imaginary instance of the couple not two years married. Oh! it can't be true – she spoke of enormous sums of money paid to this woman. I know where Arthur keeps his bank book – in one of the drawers of that desk. I might find out by that. I *will* find out. (*Opens drawer.*) No, it is some hideous mistake. (*Rises and goes C.*) Some silly scandal! He loves *me*! He loves *me*! But why should I not look? I am his wife, I have a right to look! (*Returns to bureau, takes out book and examines it page by page, smiles and gives a sigh of relief.*) I knew it! there is not a word of truth in this stupid story. (*Puts book back in drawer. As she does so, starts and takes out another book.*) A second book – private – locked! (*Tries to open it, but fails. Sees paper knife on bureau, and with it cuts cover from book. Begins to start at the first page.*) 'Mrs. Erlynne – £600 – Mrs. Erlynne – £700 – Mrs. Erlynne – £400.' Oh! it is true! It is true! How horrible! (*Throws book on floor.*)

Enter LORD WINDERMERE *C.*

Lord Windermere: Well, dear, has the fan been sent home yet? (*Going R.C. Sees book.*) Margaret, you have cut open my bank book. You have no right to do such a thing!

Lady Windermere: You think it wrong that you are found out, don't you?

Lord Windermere: I think it wrong that a wife should spy on her husband.

Lady Windermere: I did not spy on you. I never knew of this woman's existence till half an hour ago. Some one who pitied me was kind enough to tell me what every one in London knows already – your daily visits to Curzon Street, your mad infatuation, the monstrous sums of money you squander on this infamous woman! (*Crossing L.*)

Lord Windermere: Margaret! don't talk like that of Mrs. Erlynne, you don't know how unjust it is!

Lady Windermere (*turning to him*): You are very jealous of Mrs. Erlynne's honour. I wish you had been as jealous of mine.

Lord Windermere: Your honour is untouched, Margaret. You don't think for a moment that – (*Puts book back into desk.*)

Lady Windermere: I think that you spend your money strangely. That is all. Oh, don't imagine I mind about the money. As far as I am concerned you may squander everything we have. But what I *do* mind is that you who have loved me, you who have taught me to love you, should pass from the love that is given to the love that is bought. Oh, it's horrible! (*Sits on sofa.*) And it is I who feel degraded! *you* don't feel anything. I feel stained, utterly stained. You can't realise how hideous the last six months seems to me now – every kiss you have given me is tainted in my memory.

Lord Windermere (*crossing to her*): Don't say that, Margaret. I never loved any one in the whole world but you.

Lady Windermere (*rises*): Who is this woman, then? Why do you take a house for her?

Lord Windermere: I did not take a house for her.

Lady Windermere: You gave her the money to do it, which is the same thing.

Lord Windermere: Margaret, as far as I have known Mrs. Erlynne –

Lady Windermere: Is there a Mr. Erlynne – or is he a myth?

Lord Windermere: Her husband died many years ago. She is alone in the world.

Lady Windermere: No relations? (*A pause.*)

Lord Windermere: None.

Lady Windermere: Rather curious, isn't it? (*L.*)

Lord Windermere (*L.C.*): Margaret, I was saying to you – and I beg you to listen to me – that as far as I have known Mrs. Erlynne, she has conducted herself well. If years ago –

Lady Windermere: Oh! (*Crossing R.C.*) I don't want details about her life!

Lord Windermere (*C.*): I am not going to give you any details about her life. I tell you simply this – Mrs. Erlynne was once honoured, loved, respected. She was well born, she had position – she lost everything – threw it away, if you like. That makes it all the more bitter. Misfortunes one can endure – they come from outside, they are accidents. But to suffer for one's own faults – ah! – there is the sting of life. It was twenty years ago, too. She was little more than a girl then. She had been a wife for even less time than you have.

Lady Windermere: I am not interested in her – and – you should not mention this woman and me in the same breath. It is an error of taste. (*Sitting R. at desk.*)

Lord Windermere: Margaret, you could save this woman. She wants to get back into society, and she wants you to help her. (*Crossing to her.*)

Lady Windermere: Me!

Lord Windermere: Yes, you.

Lady Windermere: How impertinent of her! (*A pause.*)

Lord Windermere: Margaret, I came to ask you a great favour, and I still ask it of you, though you have discovered what I had intended you should never have known, that I have given Mrs. Erlynne a large sum of money. I want you to send her an invitation for our party to-night. (*Standing L. of her.*)

Lady Windermere: You are mad! (*Rises.*)

Lord Windermere: I entreat you. People may chatter about her, do chatter about her, of course, but they don't know anything definite against her. She has been to several houses – not to houses where you would go, I admit, but still to houses where women who are in what is called Society nowadays do go. That does not content her. She wants you to receive her once.

Lady Windermere: As a triumph for her, I suppose?

Lord Windermere: No; but because she knows that you are a good woman – and that if she comes here once she will have a chance of a happier, a surer life than she has had. She will make no further effort to know you. Won't you help a woman who is trying to get back?

Lady Windermere: No! If a woman really repents, she never wishes to return to the society that has made or seen her ruin.

Lord Windermere: I beg of you.

Lady Windermere (*crossing to door R.*): I am going to dress for dinner, and don't mention the subject again this evening. Arthur – (*going to him C.*) – you fancy because I have no father or mother that I am alone in the world, and that you can treat me as you choose. You are wrong, I have friends, many friends.

Lord Windermere (*L.C.*): Margaret, you are talking foolishly, recklessly. I won't argue with you, but I insist upon your asking Mrs. Erlynne to-night.

Lady Windermere (*R.C.*): I shall do nothing of the kind. (*Crossing L.C.*)

Lord Windermere: You refuse? (*C.*)

Lady Windermere: Absolutely!

Lord Windermere: Ah, Margaret, do this for my sake; it is her last chance.

Lady Windermere: What has that to do with me?

Lord Windermere: How hard good women are!

Lady Windermere: How weak bad men are!

Lord Windermere: Margaret, none of us men may be good enough for the women we marry – that is quite true – but you don't imagine I would ever – oh, the suggestion is monstrous!

Lady Windermere: Why should *you* be different from other men? I am told that there is hardly a husband in London who does not waste his life over *some* shameful passion.

Lord Windermere: I am not one of them.

Lady Windermere: I am not sure of that!

Lord Windermere: You are sure in your heart. But don't make chasm after chasm between us. God knows the last few minutes have thrust us wide enough apart. Sit down and write the card.

Lady Windermere: Nothing in the whole world would induce me.

Lord Windermere (*crossing to bureau*): Then I will! (*Rings electric bell, sits and writes card.*)

Lady Windermere: You are going to invite this woman? (*Crossing to him.*)

Lord Windermere: Yes.

Pause. Enter PARKER.

Parker!

Parker: Yes, my lord. (*Comes down L.C.*)

Lord Windermere: Have this note sent to Mrs. Erlynne at No. 84A Curzon Street. (*Crossing to L.C. and giving note to* PARKER.) There is no answer!

Exit PARKER *C.*

Lady Windermere: Arthur, if that woman comes here, I shall insult her.

Lord Windermere: Margaret, Don't say that.

Lady Windermere: I mean it.

Lord Windermere: Child, if you did such a thing, there's not a woman in London who wouldn't pity you.

Lady Windermere: There is not a *good* woman in London who would not applaud me. We have been too lax. We must make an example. I propose to begin to-night. (*Picking up fan.*) Yes, you gave me this fan to-day; it was your birthday present. If that woman crosses my threshold, I shall strike her across the face with it.

Lord Windermere: Margaret, you couldn't do such a thing.

Lady Windermere: You don't know me! (*Moves R.*)

Enter PARKER

Parker!

Parker: Yes, my lady.

Lady Windermere: I shall dine in my own room. I don't want dinner, in fact. See that everything is ready by half-past ten. And, Parker, be sure you pronounce the names of the guests very distinctly to-night. Sometimes you speak so fast that I miss them. I am particularly anxious to hear the names quite clearly so as to make no mistake. You understand, Parker?

Parker: Yes, my lady.

Lady Windermere: That will do!

Exit PARKER *C.*

(*Speaking to* LORD WINDERMERE): Arthur, if that woman comes here – I warn you –

Lord Windermere: Margaret, you'll ruin us!

Lady Windermere: Us! From this moment my life is separate from yours. But if you wish to avoid a public scandal, write at once to this woman, and tell her that I forbid her to come here!

Lord Windermere: I will not – I cannot – she must come!

Lady Windermere: Then I shall do exactly as I have said. (*Goes R.*) You leave me no choice. (*Exit R.*)

Lord Windermere (*calling after her*): Margaret! Margaret! (*A pause.*) My God! What shall I do? I dare not tell her who this woman really is. The shame would kill her. (*Sinks down into a chair and buries his face in his hands.*)

ACT DROP.

SECOND ACT

SCENE

Drawing-room in Lord Windermere's house. Door R.U. opening into ball-room, where band is playing. Door L. through which guests are entering. Door L. U. opens on to illuminated terrace. Palms, flowers, and brilliant lights. Room crowded with guests. Lady Windermere is receiving them.

Duchess of Berwick (up C.): So strange Lord Windermere isn't here. Mr. Hopper is very late, too. You have kept those five dances for him, Agatha? *(Comes down.)*

Lady Agatha: Yes, mamma.

Duchess of Berwick (sitting on sofa): Just let me see your card. I'm so glad Lady Windermere has revived cards. – They're a mother's only safeguard. You dear simple little thing! *(Scratches out two names.)* No nice girl should ever waltz with such particularly younger sons! It looks so fast! The last two dances you might pass on the terrace with Mr. Hopper.

Enter MR. DUMBY and LADY PLYMDALE from the ball-room.

Lady Agatha: Yes, mamma.

Duchess of Berwick (fanning herself): The air is so pleasant there.

Parker: Mrs. Cowper-Cowper. Lady Stutfield. Sir James Royston. Mr. Guy Berkeley.

These people enter as announced.

Dumby: Good evening, Lady Stutfield. I suppose this will be the last ball of the season?

Lady Stutfield: I suppose so, Mr. Dumby. It's been a delightful season, hasn't it?

Dumby: Quite delightful! Good evening, Duchess. I suppose this will be the last ball of the season?

Duchess of Berwick: I suppose so, Mr. Dumby. It has been a very dull season, hasn't it?

Dumby: Dreadfully dull! Dreadfully dull!

Mrs. Cowper-Cowper: Good evening, Mr. Dumby. I suppose this will be the last ball of the season?

Dumby: Oh, I think not. There'll probably be two more. (*Wanders back to* LADY PLYMDALE.)

Parker: Mr. Rufford. Lady Jedburgh and Miss Graham. Mr. Hopper.

These people enter as announced.

Hopper: How do you do, Lady Windermere? How do you do, Duchess? (*Bows to* LADY AGATHA.)

Duchess of Berwick: Dear Mr. Hopper, how nice of you to come so early. We all know how you are run after in London.

Hopper: Capital place, London! They are not nearly so exclusive in London as they are in Sydney.

Duchess of Berwick: Ah! we know your value, Mr. Hopper. We wish there were more like you. It would make life so much easier. Do you know, Mr. Hopper, dear Agatha and I are so much interested in Australia. It must be so pretty with all the dear little kangaroos flying about. Agatha has found it on the map. What a curious shape it is! Just like a large packing case. However, it is a very young country, isn't it?

Hopper: Wasn't it made at the same time as the others, Duchess?

Duchess of Berwick: How clever you are, Mr. Hopper. You have a cleverness quite of your own. Now I mustn't keep you.

Hopper: But I should like to dance with Lady Agatha, Duchess.

Duchess of Berwick: Well, I hope she has a dance left. Have you a dance left, Agatha?

Lady Agatha: Yes, mamma.

Duchess of Berwick: The next one?

Lady Agatha: Yes, mamma.

Hopper: May I have the pleasure? (LADY AGATHA *bows.*)

Duchess of Berwick: Mind you take great care of my little chatterbox, Mr. Hopper.

LADY AGATHA *and* MR. HOPPER *pass into ball-room.*

Enter LORD WINDERMERE *L.*

Lord Windermere: Margaret, I want to speak to you.

Lady Windermere: In a moment. (*The music stops.*)

Parker: Lord Augustus Lorton.

Enter LORD AUGUSTUS.

Lord Augustus: Good evening, Lady Windermere.
Duchess of Berwick: Sir James, will you take me into the ball-room? Augustus has been dining with us to-night. I really have had quite enough of dear Augustus for the moment.

SIR JAMES ROYSTON *gives the* DUCHESS *his arm and escorts her into the ball-room.*

Parker: Mr. and Mrs. Arthur Bowden. Lord and Lady Paisley. Lord Darlington.

These people enter as announced.

Lord Augustus (coming up to LORD WINDERMERE): Want to speak to you particularly, dear boy. I'm worn to a shadow. Know I don't look it. None of us men do look what we really are. Demmed good thing, too. What I want to know is this. Who is she? Where does she come from? Why hasn't she got any demmed relations! Demmed nuisance, relations! But they make one so demmed respectable.
Lord Windermere: You are talking of Mrs. Erlynne, I suppose? I only met her six months ago. Till then, I never knew of her existence.
Lord Augustus: You have seen a good deal of her since then.
Lord Windermere (coldly): Yes, I have seen a good deal of her since then. I have just seen her.
Lord Augustus: Egad! the women are very down on her. I have been dining with Arabella this evening! By Jove! you should have heard what she said about Mrs. Erlynne. She didn't leave a rag on her. . . . *(Aside.)* Berwick and I told her that didn't matter much, as the lady in question must have an extremely fine figure. You should have seen Arabella's expression. . . But, look here, dear boy. I don't know what to do about Mrs. Erlynne. Egad! I might be married to her; she treats me with such demmed indifference. She's deuced clever, too! She explains everything. Egad! she explains you. She has got any amount of explanations for you – and all of them different.
Lord Windermere: No explanations are necessary about my friendship with Mrs. Erlynne.

Lord Augustus: Hem! Well, look here, dear old fellow. Do you think she will ever get into this demmed thing called Society? Would you introduce her to your wife? No use beating about the confounded bush. Would you do that?

Lord Windermere: Mrs. Erlynne is coming here to-night.

Lord Augustus: Your wife has sent her a card?

Lord Windermere: Mrs. Erlynne has received a card.

Lord Augustus: Then she's all right, dear boy. But why didn't you tell me that before? It would have saved me a heap of worry and demmed mis-understandings!

LADY AGATHA *and* MR. HOPPER *cross and exit on terrace* L.U.E.

Parker: Mr. Cecil Graham!

Enter MR. CECIL GRAHAM.

Cecil Graham (*bows to* LADY WINDERMERE, *passes over and shakes hands with* LORD WINDERMERE): Good evening, Arthur. Why don't you ask me how I am? I like people to ask me how I am. It shows a wide-spread interest in my health. Now, to-night I am not at all well. Been dining with my people. Wonder why it is one's people are always so tedious? My father would talk morality after dinner. I told him he was old enough to know better. But my experience is that as soon as people are old enough to know better, they don't know anything at all. Hullo, Tuppy! Hear you're going to be married again; thought you were tired of that game.

Lord Augustus: You're excessively trivial, my dear boy, excessively trivial!

Cecil Graham: By the way, Tuppy, which is it? Have you been twice married and once divorced, or twice divorced and once married? I say you've been twice divorced and once married. It seems so much more probable.

Lord Augustus: I have a very bad memory. I really don't remember which. (*Moves away R.*)

Lady Plymdale: Lord Windermere, I've something most particular to ask you.

Lord Windermere: I am afraid – if you will excuse me – I must join my wife.

Lady Plymdale: Oh, you mustn't dream of such a thing. It's most dangerous nowadays for a husband to pay any attention to his wife in public. It always makes people think that he beats her when they're alone. The world has grown so suspicious of anything that looks like a happy married life. But I'll tell you what it is at supper. (*Moves towards door of ball-room.*)

Lord Windermere (*C.*): Margaret! I *must* speak to you.

Lady Windermere: Will you hold my fan for me, Lord Darlington? Thanks. (*Comes down to him.*)

Lord Windermere (*crossing to her*): Margaret, what you said before dinner was, of course, impossible?

Lady Windermere: That woman is not coming here to-night.

Lord Windermere (*R.C.*): Mrs. Erlynne is coming here, and if you in any way annoy or wound her, you will bring shame and sorrow on us both. Remember that! Ah, Margaret, only trust me! A wife should trust her husband!

Lady Windermere (*C.*): London is full of women who trust their husbands. One can always recognise them. They look so thoroughly unhappy. I am not going to be one of them. (*Moves up.*) Lord Darlington, will you give me back my fan please? Thanks. . . . A useful thing a fan, isn't it ? . . . I want a friend to-night, Lord Darlington; I didn't know I would want one so soon.

Lord Darlington: Lady Windermere! I knew the time would come some day; but why to-night?

Lord Windermere: I will tell her. I must. It would be terrible if there were any scene. Margaret. . .

Parker: Mrs. Erlynne!

LORD WINDERMERE *starts*. MRS. ERLYNNE *enters, very beautifully dressed and very dignified.* LADY WINDERMERE *clutches at her fan, then lets it drop on the floor. She bows coldly to* MRS. ERLYNNE, *who bows to her sweetly in turn, and sails into the room.*

Lord Darlington: You have dropped your fan, Lady Windermere. (*Picks it up and hands it to her.*)

Mrs. Erlynne (*C.*): How do you do, again, Lord Windermere? How charming your sweet wife looks! Quite a picture!

Lord Windermere (*in a low voice*): It was terribly rash of you to come!

Mrs. Erlynne (*smiling*): The wisest thing I ever did in my life. And, by the way, you must pay me a good deal of attention this evening. I am afraid of the women. You must introduce me to some of them. The men I can always manage. How do you do, Lord Augustus? You have quite neglected me lately. I have not seen you since yesterday. I am afraid you're faithless. Every one told me so.

Augustus (R.): Now really, Mrs. Erlynne, allow me to

Erlynne (R.C.): No, dear Lord Augustus, you can't explain anything. It is your chief charm.

Lord Augustus: Ah! if you find charms in me, Mrs. Erlynne –

They converse together. LORD WINDERMERE *moves uneasily about the room watching* MRS. ERLYNNE.

Lord Darlington (to Lady Winermere): How pale you are!

Lady Windermere: Cowards are always pale!

Lord Darlington: You look faint. Come out on the terrace.

Lady Windermere: Yes. (*To* PARKER): Parker, send my cloak out.

Mrs. Erlynne (crossing to her): Lady Windermere, how beautifully your terrace is illuminated. Reminds me of Prince Doria's at Rome.

LADY WINDERMERE *bows coldly, and goes out with* LORD DARLINGTON.

Oh, how do you do, Mr. Graham? Isn't that your aunt, Lady Jedburgh? I should so much like to know her.

Cecil Graham (after a moment's hesitation and embarrassment): Oh, certainly, if you wish it. Aunt Caroline, allow me to introduce Mrs. Erlynne.

Mrs. Erlynne: So pleased to meet you, Lady Jedburgh. (*Sits beside her on the sofa.*) Your nephew and I are great friends. I am so much interested in his political career. I think he's sure to be a wonderful success. He thinks like a Tory, and talks like a Radical, and that's so important nowadays. He's such a brilliant talker, too. But we all know from whom he inherits that. Lord Allandale was saying to me only yesterday, in the park, that Mr. Graham talks almost as well as his aunt.

Lady Jedburgh (R.): Most kind of you to say these charming things to me! (MRS. ERLYNNE *smiles, and continues conversation.*)

Dumby (to CECIL GRAHAM): Did you introduce Mrs. Erlynne to Lady Jedburgh?

Cecil Graham: Had to, my dear fellow. Couldn't help it! That woman can make one do anything she wants. How, I don't know.

Dumby: Hope to goodness she won't speak to me! (*Saunters towards* LADY PLYMDALE.)

Mrs. Erlynne (C. To LADY JEDBURGH): On Thursday? With great pleasure. (*Rises, and speaks to* LORD WINDERMERE, *laugh-*

ing.) What a bore it is to have to be civil to these old dowagers! But they always insist on it!

Lady Plymdale (*to* MR. DUMBY): Who is that well-dressed woman talking to Windermere?

Dumby: Haven't got the slightest idea! Looks like an *édition de luxe* of a wicked French novel, meant specially for the English market.

Mrs. Erlynne: So that is poor Dumby with Lady Plymdale? I hear she is frightfully jealous of him. He doesn't seem anxious to speak to me to-night. I suppose he is afraid of her. Those straw-coloured women have dreadful tempers. Do you know, I think I'll dance with you first, Windermere. (LORD WINDERMERE *bites his lip and frowns.*) It will make Lord Augustus so jealous! Lord Augustus! (LORD AUGUSTUS *comes down.*) Lord Windermere insists on my dancing with him first, and, as it's his own house, I can't well refuse. You know I would much sooner dance with you.

Lord Augustus (*with a low bow*): I wish I could think so, Mrs. Erlynne.

Mrs. Erlynne: You know it far too well. I can fancy a person dancing through life with you and finding it charming.

Lord Augustus (*placing his hand on his white waistcoat*): Oh, thank you, thank you. You are the most adorable of all ladies!

Mrs. Erlynne: What a nice speech! So simple and so sincere! Just the sort of speech I like. Well, you shall hold my bouquet. (*Goes towards ball-room on* LORD WINDERMERE'S *arm.*) Ah, Mr. Dumby, how are you? I am so sorry I have been out the last three times you have called. Come and lunch on Friday.

Dumby (*with perfect nonchalance*): Delighted!

LADY PLYMDALE *glares with indignation at* MR. DUMBY. LORD AUGUSTUS *follows* MRS. ERLYNNE *and* LORD WINDERMERE *into the ball-room holding bouquet.*

Lady Plymdale (*to* MR. DUMBY): What an absolute brute you are! I never can believe a word you say! Why did you tell me you didn't know her? What do you mean by calling on her three times running? You are not to go to lunch there; of course you understand that?

Dumby: My dear Laura, I wouldn't dream of going!

Lady Plymdale: You haven't told me her name yet! Who is she?

Dumby (*coughs slightly and smooths his hair*): She's a Mrs. Erlynne.

Lady Plymdale: That woman!

Dumby: Yes. that is what every one calls her.

Lady Plymdale: How very interesting! How intensely interesting! I really must have a good stare at her. (*Goes to door of ball-room and looks in.*) I have heard the most shocking things about her. They say she is ruining poor Windermere. And Lady Windermere, who goes in for being so proper, invites her! How extremely amusing! It takes a thoroughly good woman to do a thoroughly stupid thing. You are to lunch there on Friday!

Dumby: Why?

Lady Plymdale: Because I want you to take my husband with you. He has been so attentive lately, that he has become a perfect nuisance. Now, this woman is just the thing for him. He'll dance attendance upon her as long as she lets him, and won't bother me. I assure you, women of that kind are most useful. They form the basis of other people's marriages.

Dumby: What a mystery you are!

Lady Plymdale (*looking at him*): I wish *you* were!

Dumby: I am – to myself. I am the only person in the world I should like to know thoroughly; but I don't see any chance of it just at present.

They pass into the ball-room, and LADY WINDERMERE *and* LORD DARLINGTON *enter from the terrace.*

Lady Windermere: Yes. Yes. Her coming here is monstrous, unbearable. I know now what you meant to-day at tea time. Why didn't you tell me right out? You should have!

Lord Darlington: I couldn't! A man can't tell these things about another man! But if I had known he was going to make you ask her here to-night, I think I would have told you. That insult, at any rate, you would have been spared.

Lady Windermere: I did not ask her. He insisted on her coming – against my entreaties – against my commands. Oh! the house is tainted for me! I feel that every woman here sneers at me as she dances by with my husband. What have I done to deserve this? I gave him all my life. He took it – used it – spoiled it! I am degraded in my own eyes, and I lack courage – I am a coward! (*Sits down on sofa.*)

Lord Darlington: If I know you at all, I know that you can't live with a man who treats you like this! What sort of life would you have with him? You would feel that he was lying to you every moment of the day. You would feel that the look in his eyes was false, his voice false, his touch false, his passion false. He would come to you when he was weary of others; you would have to comfort him. He would come to you when he was devoted to others; you would have to charm him. You would have to be to him the mask of his real life, the cloak to hide his secret.

Lady Windermere: You are right – you are terribly right. But where am I to turn? You said you would be my friend, Lord Darlington. – Tell me, what am I to do? Be my friend now.

Lord Darlington: Between men and women there is no friendship possible. There is passion, enmity, worship, love, but no friendship. I love you –

Lady Windermere: No, no! (*Rises.*)

Lord Darlington: Yes, I love you! You are more to me than anything in the whole world. What does your husband give you? Nothing. Whatever is in him he gives to this wretched woman, whom he has thrust into your society, into your home, to shame you before every one. I offer you my life –

Lady Windermere: Lord Darlington!

Lord Darlington: My life – my whole life. Take it, and do with it what you will. . . . I love you – love you as I have never loved any living thing. From the moment I met you I loved you, loved you blindly, adoringly, madly! You did not know it then – you know it now! Leave this house to-night. I won't tell you that the world matters nothing, or the world's voice, or the voice of society. They matter a great deal. They matter far too much. But there are moments when one has to choose between living one's own life, fully, entirely, completely – or dragging out some false shallow, degrading existence that the world in its hypocrisy demands. You have that moment now. Choose! Oh, my love, choose.

Lady Windermere (*moving slowly away from him, and looking at him with startled eyes*): I have not the courage.

Lord Darlington (*following her*): Yes; you have the courage. There may be six months of pain, of disgrace even, but when you no longer bear his name, when you bear mine, all will be well. Margaret, my love, my wife that shall be some day – yes, my wife! You know it! What are you now? This woman has the place that belongs by right to you. Oh! go – go out of this house, with head erect, with a smile upon your lips, with courage in your eyes. All London will know why you did it; and who will blame you? No one. If they do, what matter? Wrong? What is wrong? It's wrong for a man to abandon his wife for a shameless woman. It is wrong for a wife to remain with a man who so dishonours her. You said once you would make no compromise with things. Make none now. Be brave! Be yourself!

Lady Windermere: I am afraid of being myself. Let me think. Let me wait! My husband may return to me. (*Sits down on sofa.*)

Lord Darlington: And you would take him back! You are not what I thought you were. You are just the same as every other woman. You would stand anything rather than face the censure of a world, whose praise you would despise. In a week you will be driving with this woman in the Park. She will be your constant guest – your dearest friend. You would endure anything rather than break with one blow this monstrous tie. You are right. You have no courage; none!

Lady Windermere: Ah, give me time to think. I cannot answer you now. (*Passes her hand nervously over her brow.*)

Lord Darlington: It must be now or not at all.

Lady Windermere (rising from the sofa): Then, not at all! (*A pause.*)

Lord Darlington: You break my heart!

Lady Windermere: Mine is already broken. (*A pause.*)

Lord Darlington: To-morrow I leave England. This is the last time I shall ever look on you. You will never see me again. For one moment our lives met – our souls touched. They must never meet or touch again. Good-bye, Margaret. (*Exit.*)

Lady Windermere: How alone I am in life. How terribly alone!

The music stops. Enter the DUCHESS OF BERWICK *and* LORD PAISLEY *laughing and talking. Other guests come in from ball-room.*

Duchess of Berwick: Dear Margaret, I've just been having such a delightful chat with Mrs. Erlynne. I am so sorry for what I said to you this afternoon about her. Of course, she must be all right if *you* invite her. A most attractive woman, and has such sensible views on life. Told me she entirely disapproved of people marrying more than once, so I feel quite safe about poor Augustus. Can't imagine why people speak against her. It's those horrid nieces of mine – the Saville girls – they're always talking scandal. Still, I should go to Homburg, dear, I really should. She is just a little too attractive. But where is Agatha? Oh there she is. (LADY AGATHA *and* MR. HOPPER *enter from terrace L.U.E.*) Mr. Hopper, I am very very angry with you. You have taken Agatha out on the terrace, and she is so delicate.

Hopper (L.C.): Awfully sorry, Duchess. We went out for a moment and then got chatting together.

Duchess of Berwick (C.): Ah, about dear Australia, I suppose?
Hopper: Yes!
Duchess of Berwick: Agatha, darling! (*Beckons her over.*)
Lady Agatha: Yes, mamma!
Duchess of Berwick (aside): Did Mr. Hopper definitely –
Lady Agatha: Yes, mamma.
Duchess of Berwick: And what answer did you give him, dear child?
Lady Agatha: Yes, mamma.
Duchess of Berwick (affectionately): My dear one! You always say the right thing. Mr. Hopper! James! Agatha has told me everything. How cleverly you have both kept your secret.
Hopper: You don't mind my taking Agatha off to Australia, then, Duchess?
Duchess of Berwick (indignantly): To Australia? Oh, don't mention that dreadful vulgar place.
Hopper: But she said she'd like to come with me.
Duchess of Berwick (severely): Did you say that, Agatha?
Lady Agatha: Yes, mamma.
Duchess of Berwick: Agatha, you say the most silly things possible. I think on the whole that Grosvenor Square would be a more healthy place to reside in. There are lots of vulgar people live in Grosvenor Square, but at any rate there are no horrid kangaroos crawling about. But we'll talk about that to-morrow. James, you can take Agatha down. You'll come to lunch, of course, James. At half-past one, instead of two. The Duke will wish to say a few words to you, I am sure.
Hopper: I should like to have a chat with the Duke, Duchess. He has not said a single word to me yet.
Duchess of Berwick: I think you'll find he will have a great deal to say to you to-morrow. (*Exit* LADY AGATHA *with* MR. HOPPER.) And now good-night Margaret. I'm afraid it's the old, old story, dear. Love – well, not love at first sight, but love at the end of the season, which is so much more satisfactory.
Lady Windermere: Good-night, Duchess.

Exit the DUCHESS OF BERWICK *on* LORD PAISLEY'S *arm.*

Lady Plymdale: My dear Margaret, what a handsome woman your husband has been dancing with! I should be quite jealous if I were you! Is she a great friend of yours?
Lady Windermere: No!
Lady Plymdale: Really? Good-night, dear. (*Looks at* MR. DUMBY *and exit.*)

Dumby: Awful manners young Hopper has!

Cecil Graham: Ah! Hopper is one of Nature's gentlemen, the worst type of gentleman I know.

Dumby: Sensible woman, Lady Windermere. Lots of wives would have objected to Mrs. Erlynne coming. But Lady Windermere has that uncommon thing called common sense.

Cecil Graham: And Windermere knows that nothing looks so like innocence as an indiscretion.

Dumby: Yes; dear Windermere is becoming almost modern. Never thought he would. (*Bows to* LADY WINDERMERE *and exit.*)

Lady Jedburgh: Good-night, Lady Windermere. What a fascinating woman Mrs. Erlynne is! She is coming to lunch on Thursday, won't you come too? I expect the Bishop and dear Lady Merton.

Lady Windermere: I am afraid I am engaged, Lady Jedburgh.

Lady Jedburgh: So sorry. Come, dear.

Exeunt LADY JEDBURGH *and* MISS GRAHAM.
Enter MRS. ERLYNNE *and* LORD WINDERMERE.

Mrs. Erlynne: Charming ball it has been! Quite reminds me of old days. (*Sits on sofa.*) And I see that there are just as many fools in society as there used to be. So pleased to find that nothing has altered! Except Margaret. She's grown quite pretty. The last time I saw her – twenty years ago, she was a fright in flannel. Positive fright, I assure you. The dear Duchess! and that sweet Lady Agatha! Just the type of girl I like! Well, really, Windermere, if I am to be the Duchess's sister-in-law –

Lord Windermere (*sitting L. of her*): But are you – ?

Exit MR. CECIL GRAHAM *with rest of guests.* LADY WINDERMERE *watches, with a look of scorn and pain,* MRS. ERLYNNE *and her husband. They are unconscious of her presence.*

Mrs. Erlynne: Oh, yes! He's to call to-morrow at twelve o'clock! He wanted to propose to-night. In fact he did. He kept on proposing. Poor Augustus, you know how he repeats himself. Such a bad habit! But I told him I wouldn't give him an answer till to-morrow. Of course I am going to take him. And I dare say I'll make him an admirable wife, as wives go. And there is a great deal of good in Lord Augustus. Fortunately it is all on the surface. Just where good qualities should be. Of course you must help me in this matter.

Lord Windermere: I am not called on to encourage Lord Augustus, I suppose?

Mrs. Erlynne: Oh, no! I do the encouraging. But you will make me a handsome settlement, Windermere, won't you?

Lord Windermere (frowning): Is that what you want to talk to me about to-night?

Mrs. Erlynne: Yes.

Lord Windermere (with a gesture of impatience): I will not talk of it here.

Mrs. Erlynne (laughing): Then we will talk of it on the terrace. Even business should have a picturesque background. Should it not, Windermere? With a proper background women can do anything.

Lord Windermere: Won't to-morrow do as well?

Mrs. Erlynne: No; you see, to-morrow I am going to accept him. And I think it would be a good thing if I was able to tell him that I had – well, what shall I say? – £2000 a year left to me by a third cousin – or a second husband – or some distant relative of that kind. It would be an additional attraction, wouldn't it? You have a delightful opportunity now of paying me a compliment, Windermere. But you are not very clever at paying compliments. I am afraid Margaret doesn't encourage you in that excellent habit. It's a great mistake on her part. When men give up saying what is charming, they give up thinking what is charming. But seriously, what do you say to £2000? £2500, I think. In modern life margin is everything. Windermere, don't you think the world an intensely amusing place? I do!

Exit on terrace with LORD WINDERMERE. *Music strikes up in ball-room.*

Lady Windermere: To stay in this house any longer is impossible. To-night a man who loves me offered me his whole life. I refused it. It was foolish of me. I will offer him mine now. I will give him mine. I will go to him! (*Puts on cloak and goes to the door, then turns back. Sits down at table and writes a letter, puts it into an envelope, and leaves it on table.*) Arthur has never understood me. When he reads this, he will. He may do as he chooses now with his life. I have done with mine as I think best, as I think right. It is he who has broken the bond of marriage – not I. I only break its bondage. (*Exit.*)

PARKER *enters L. and crosses towards the ballroom R. Enter* MRS. ERLYNNE.

Mrs. Erlynne: Is Lady Windermere in the ballroom?

Parker: Her ladyship has just gone out.

Mrs. Erlynne: Gone out? She's not on the terrace?

Parker: No, madam. Her ladyship has just gone out of the house.

Mrs. Erlynne (starts, and looks at the servant with a puzzled expression in her face): Out of the house?

Parker: Yes, madam – her ladyship told me she had left a letter for his lordship on the table.

Mrs. Erlynne: A letter for Lord Windermere?

Parker: Yes, madam.

Mrs. Erlynne: Thank you.

Exit PARKER. *The music in the ball-room stops.*

Gone out of her house! A letter addressed to her husband! (*Goes over to bureau and looks at letter. Takes it up and lays it down again with a shudder of fear.*) No, no! It would be impossible! Life doesn't repeat its tragedies like that! Oh, why does this horrible fancy come across me? Why do I remember now the one moment of my life I most wish to forget? Does life repeat its tragedies? (*Tears letter open and reads it, then sinks down into a chair with a gesture of anguish.*) Oh, how terrible! The same words that twenty years ago I wrote to her father! and how bitterly I have been punished for it! No, my punishment, my real punishment is to-night, is now! (*Still seated R.*)

Enter LORD WINDERMERE *L.U.E.*

Lord Windermere: Have you said good-night to my wife? (*Comes C.*)

Mrs. Erlynne (crushing letter in her hand): Yes.

Lord Windermere: Where is she?

Mrs. Erlynne: She is very tired. She has gone to bed. She said she had a headache.

Lord Windermere: I must go to her. You'll excuse me?

Mrs. Erlynne (rising hurriedly): Oh, no! It's nothing serious. She's only very tired, that is all. Besides, there are people still in the supper-room. She wants you to make her apologies to them. She said she didn't wish to be disturbed. (*Drops letter.*) She asked me to tell you!

Lord Windermere (picks up letter): You have dropped something.

Mrs. Erlynne: Oh yes, thank you, that is mine. (*Puts out her hand to take it.*)

Lord Windermere (*still looking at letter*): But it's my wife's handwriting, isn't it?

Mrs. Erlynne (*takes the letter quickly*): Yes, it's – an address. Will you ask them to call my carriage, please?

Lord Windermere: Certainly. (*Goes L. and Exit.*)

Mrs. Erlynne: Thanks! What can I do? What can I do? I feel a passion awakening within me that I never felt before. What can it mean? The daughter must not be like the mother – that would be terrible. How can I save her? How can I save my child? A moment may ruin a life. Who knows that better than I? Windermere must be got out of the house; that is absolutely necessary. (*Goes L.*) But how shall I do it? It must be done somehow. Ah!

Enter LORD AUGUSTUS *R.U.E. carrying bouquet.*

Lord Augustus: Dear lady, I am in such suspense! May I not have an answer to my request?

Mrs. Erlynne: Lord Augustus, listen to me. You are to take Lord Windermere down to your club at once, and keep him there as long as possible. You understand?

Lord Augustus: But you said you wished me to keep early hours!

Mrs. Erlynne (*nervously*): Do what I tell you. Do what I tell you.

Lord Augustus: And my reward?

Mrs. Erlynne: Your reward? Your reward? Oh! ask me that to-morrow. But don't let Windermere out of your sight to-night. If you do I will never forgive you. I will never speak to you again. I'll have nothing to do with you. Remember you are to keep Windermere at your club, and don't let him come back to-night. (*Exit L.*)

Lord Augustus: Well, really, I might be her husband already, positively I might. (*Follows her in a bewildered manner.*)

ACT DROP.

THIRD ACT

SCENE

Lord Darlington's rooms. A large sofa is in front of fireplace R. At the back of the stage a curtain is drawn across the window. Doors L. and R. Table R. with writing materials. Table C. with syphons, glasses, and Tantalus frame. Table L. with cigar and cigarette box. Lamps lit.

Lady Windermere (*standing by the fireplace*): Why doesn't he come? This waiting is horrible. He should be here. Why is he not here, to wake by passionate words some fire within me? I am cold – cold as a loveless thing. Arthur must have read my letter by this time. If he cared for me, he would have come after me, would have taken me back by force. But he doesn't care. He's entrammelled by this woman – fascinated by her – dominated by her. If a woman wants to hold a man, she has merely to appeal to what is worst in him. We make gods of men and they leave us. Others make brutes of them and they fawn and are faithful. How hideous life is! . . . Oh! it was mad of me to come here, horribly mad. And yet, which is the worst, I wonder, to be at the mercy of a man who loves one, or the wife of a man who in one's own house dishonours one? What woman knows? What woman in the whole world? But will he love me always, this man to whom I am giving my life? What do I bring him? Lips that have lost the note of joy, eyes that are blinded by tears, chill hands and icy heart. I bring him nothing. I must go back – no; I can't go back, my letter has put me in their power – Arthur would not take me back! That fatal letter! No! Lord Darlington leaves England to-morrow. I will go with him – I have no choice. (*Sits down for a few moments. Then starts up and puts on her cloak.*) No, no! I will go back, let Arthur do with me what he pleases. I can't wait here. It has been madness my coming. I must go at once. As for Lord Darlington. – Oh! here he is! What shall I do? What can I say to him? Will he let me go away at all? I have heard that men are brutal, horrible. . . . Oh! (*Hides her face in her hands.*)

Enter MRS. ERLYNNE *L.*

Mrs. Erlynne: Lady Windermere! (LADY WINDERMERE *starts and looks up. Then recoils in contempt.*) Thank Heaven I am in time. You must go back to your husband's house immediately.

Lady Windermere: Must?

Mrs. Erlynne (authoritatively): Yes, you must! There is not a second to be lost. Lord Darlington may return at any moment.

Lady Windermere: Don't come near me!

Mrs. Erlynne: Oh! You are on the brink of ruin, you are on the brink of a hideous precipice. You must leave this place at once, my carriage is waiting at the corner of the street. You must come with me and drive straight home.

LADY WINDERMERE *throws off her cloak and flings it on the sofa.*

What are you doing?

Lady Windermere: Mrs. Erlynne – if you had not come here, I would have gone back. But now that I see you, I feel that nothing in the whole world would induce me to live under the same roof as Lord Windermere. You fill me with horror. There is something about you that stirs the wildest – rage within me. And I know why you are here. My husband sent you to lure me back that I might serve as a blind to whatever relations exist between you and him.

Mrs. Erlynne: Oh! You don't think that – you can't.

Lady Windermere: Go back to my husband, Mrs Erlynne. He belongs to you and not to me. I suppose he is afraid of a scandal. Men are such cowards. They outrage every law of the world, and are afraid of the world's tongue. But he had better prepare himself. He shall have a scandal. He shall have the worst scandal there has been in London for years. He shall see his name in every vile paper, mine on every hideous placard.

Mrs. Erlynne: No – no –

Lady Windermere: Yes! he shall. Had he come himself, I admit I would have gone back to the life of degradation you and he had prepared for me – I was going back – but to stay himself at home, and to send you as his messenger – oh! it was infamous – infamous.

Mrs. Erlynne (C.): Lady Windermere, you wrong me horribly – you wrong your husband horribly. He doesn't know you are here – he thinks you are safe in your own house. He thinks you are asleep in your own room. He never read the mad letter you wrote to him!

Lady Windermere (R.): Never read it!

Mrs. Erlynne: No – he knows nothing about it.

Lady Windermere: How simple you think me! (*Going to her.*) You are lying to me!

Mrs. Erlynne (*restraining herself*): I am not. I am telling you the truth.

Lady Windermere: If my husband didn't read my letter, how is it that you are here? Who told you I had left the house you were shameless enough to enter? Who told you where I had gone to? My husband told you, and sent you to decoy me back. (*Crosses L.*)

Mrs. Erlynne (*R.C.*): You husband has never seen the letter. I – saw it, I opened it. I – read it.

Lady Windermere (*turning to her*): You opened a letter of mine to my husband? You wouldn't dare!

Mrs. Erlynne: Dare! Oh! to save you from the abyss into which you are falling, there is nothing in the world I would not dare, nothing in the whole world. Here is the letter. Your husband has never read it. He never shall read it. (*Going to fireplace.*) It should never have been written. (*Tears it and throws it into the fire.*)

Lady Windermere (*with infinite contempt in her voice and look*): How do I know that that was my letter after all? You seem to think the commonest device can take me in!

Mrs. Erlynne: Oh! why do you disbelieve everything I tell you? What object do you think I have in coming here, except to save you from utter ruin, to save you from the consequence of a hideous mistake? That letter that is burnt now was your letter. I swear it to you!

Lady Windermere (*slowly*): You took good care to burn it before I had examined it. I cannot trust you. You, whose whole life is a lie, how could you speak the truth about anything? (*Sits down.*)

Mrs. Erlynne (*hurriedly*): Think as you like about me – say what you choose against me, but go back, go back to the husband you love.

Lady Windermere (*sullenly*): I do *not* love him!

Mrs. Erlynne: You do, and you know that he loves you.

Lady Windermere: He does not understand what love is. He understands it as little as you do – but I see what you want. It would be a great advantage for you to get me back. Dear Heaven! what a life I would have then! Living at the mercy of a woman who has neither mercy nor pity in her, a woman whom it is an infamy to meet, a degradation to know, a vile woman, a woman who comes between husband and wife!

Mrs. Erlynne (*with a gesture of despair*): Lady Windermere, Lady Windermere, don't say such terrible things. You don't know how terrible they are, how terrible and how unjust. Listen, you must listen! Only go back to your husband, and I promise you never to communicate with him again on any pretext – never to see him – never to have anything to do with his life or yours. The money that he gave me, he gave me not through love, but through hatred, not in worship, but in contempt. The hold I have over him –

Lady Windermere (rising): Ah! you admit you have a hold!

Mrs. Erlynne: Yes, and I will tell you what it is. It is his love for you, Lady Windermere.

Lady Windermere: You expect me to believe that?

Mrs. Erlynne: You must believe it! it is true. It is his love for you that has made him submit to – oh! call it what you like, tyranny, threats, anything you choose. But it is his love for you. His desire to spare you – shame, yes, shame and disgrace.

Lady Windermere: What do you mean? You are insolent! What have I to do with you?

Mrs. Erlynne (humbly): Nothing. I know it – but I tell you that your husband loves you – that you may never meet with such love again in your whole life – that such love you will never meet – and that if you throw it away, the day may come when you will starve for love and it will not be given to you, beg for love and it will be denied you. – Oh! Arthur loves you!

Lady Windermere: Arthur? And you tell me there is nothing between you?

Mrs. Erlynne: Lady Windermere, before Heaven your husband is guiltless of all offence towards you! And I – I tell you that had it ever occurred to me that such a monstrous suspicion would have entered your mind, I would have died rather than have crossed your life or his – oh! died, gladly died! (*Moves away to sofa R.*)

Lady Windermere: You talk as if you had a heart. Women like you have no hearts. Heart is not in you. You are bought and sold. (*Sits L.C.*)

Mrs. Erlynne (starts, with a gesture of pain. Then restrains herself, and comes over to where Lady Windermere is sitting. As she speaks, she stretches out her hands towards her, but does not dare to touch her): Believe what you choose about me. I am not worth a moment's sorrow. But don't spoil your beautiful young life on my account! You don't know what may be in store for you, unless you leave this house at once. You don't know what it is to fall into the pit, to be despised, mocked, abandoned, sneered at – to be an outcast! to find the door shut against one, to have to creep in by hideous byways, afraid every moment lest the mask should be stripped from one's face, and all the while to hear the laughter, the horrible laughter of the world, a thing more tragic than all the tears the world has ever shed. You don't know what it is. One pays for one's sin, and then one pays again, and all one's life one pays. You must never know that. – As for me, if suffering be an expiation, then at this moment I have expiated all my faults, whatever they have been; for to-night you have made a heart in one who had it not, made it and broken it. – But let that pass. I may have wrecked my own life, but I will not let you wreck yours. You – why, you are a mere girl, you would be lost. You haven't got the kind of brains that enables a woman to get back. You have neither the wit nor the courage. You couldn't stand dishonour! No! Go back, Lady Windermere, to the husband who loves you, whom you love. You have a child, Lady Windermere. Go back to that child who even now, in pain or in joy, may be calling to you. (LADY WINDER-MERE *rises.*) God gave you that child. He will require from you that you make his life fine, that you watch over him. What answer will you make to God if his life is ruined through you? Back to your house, Lady Windermere – your husband loves you! He has never swerved for a moment from the love he bears you. But even if he had a thousand loves, you must stay with your child. If he was harsh to you, you must stay with your child. If he ill-treated you, you must stay with your child. If he abandoned you, your place is with your child.

LADY WINDERMERE *bursts into tears and buries her face in her hands.*

(*Rushing to he.*): Lady Windermere!
Lady Windermere (*holding out her hands to her helplessly, as a child might do*): Take me home. Take me home.
Mrs. Erlynne (*is about to embrace her. Then restrains herself. There is a look of wonderful joy in her face*): Come! Where is your cloak? (*Getting it from sofa*): Here. Put it on. Come at once!

They go to the door.

Lady Windermere: Stop! Don't you hear voices?
Mrs. Erlynne: No, no! There is no one!
Lady Windermere: Yes, there is! Listen! Oh! that is my husband's voice! He is coming in! Save me! Oh, it's some plot! You have sent for him.

Voices outside.

Mrs. Erlynne: Silence! I'm here to save you, if I can. But I fear it is too late! There! (*Points to the curtain across the window.*) The first chance you have slip out, if you ever get a chance!

Lady Windermere: But you?

Mrs. Erlynne: Oh! never mind me. I'll face them.

LADY WINDERMERE *hides herself behind the curtain.*

Lord Augustus (outside): Nonsense, dear Windermere, you must not leave me!

Mrs. Erlynne: Lord Augustus! Then it is I who am lost! (*Hesitates for a moment, then looks round and sees door R., and exit through it.*)

Enter LORD DARLINGTON, MR. DUMBY, LORD WINDERMERE, LORD AUGUSTUS LORTON, *and* MR. CECIL GRAHAM.

Dumby: What a nuisance their turning us out of the club at this hour! It's only two o'clock. (*Sinks into a chair.*) The lively part of the evening is only just beginning. (*Yawns and closes his eyes.*)

Lord Windermere: It is very good of you, Lord Darlington, allowing Augustus to force our company on you, but I'm afraid I can't stay long.

Lord Darlington: Really! I am so sorry! You'll take a cigar, won't you?

Lord Windermere: Thanks! (*Sits down.*)

Lord Augustus (to LORD WINDERMERE*):* My dear boy, you must not dream of going. I have a great deal to talk to you about, of demmed importance, too. (*Sits down with him at L. table.*)

Cecil Graham: Oh! We all know what that is! Tuppy can't talk about anything but Mrs. Erlynne.

Lord Windermere: Well, that is no business of yours, is it, Cecil?

Cecil Graham: None! That is why it interests me. My own business always bores me to death. I prefer other people's.

Lord Darlington: Have something to drink, you fellows. Cecil, you'll have a whisky and soda?

Cecil Graham: Thanks. (*Goes to table with* LORD DARLINGTON.*) Mrs. Erlynne looked very handsome to-night, didn't she?

Lord Darlington: I am not one of her admirers.

Cecil Graham: I usen't to be, but I am now. Why! she actually made me introduce her to poor dear Aunt Caroline. I believe she is going to lunch there.

Lord Darlington (*in surprise*): No?

Cecil Graham: She is, really.

Lord Darlington: Excuse me, you fellows. I'm going away to-morrow. And I have to write a few letters. (*Goes to writing-table and sits down.*)

Dumby: Clever woman, Mrs. Erlynne.

Cecil Graham: Hallo, Dumby! I thought you were asleep.

Dumby: I am, I usually am!

Lord Augustus: A very clever woman. Knows perfectly well what a demmed fool I am – knows it as well as I do myself.

CECIL GRAHAM *comes towards him laughing.*

Ah, you may laugh, my boy, but it is a great thing to come across a woman who thoroughly understands one.

Dumby: It is an awfully dangerous thing. They always end by marrying one.

Cecil Graham: But I thought, Tuppy, you were never going to see her again! Yes! you told me so yesterday evening at the club. You said you'd heard –

Whispering to him.

Lord Augustus: Oh, she's explained that.

Cecil Graham: And the Wiesbaden affair?

Lord Augustus: She's explained that too.

Dumby: And her income, Tuppy? Has she explained that?

Lord Augustus (*in a very serious voice*): She's going to explain that to-morrow.

CECIL GRAHAM *goes back to C. table.*

Dumby: Awfully commercial, women nowadays. Our grandmothers threw their caps over the mills, of course, but, by Jove, their grand-daughters only throw their caps over mills that can raise the wind for them.

Lord Augustus: You want to make her out a wicked woman. She is not!

Cecil Graham: Oh! Wicked women bother one. Good women bore one. That is the only difference between them.

Lord Augustus (*puffing a cigar*): Mrs. Erlynne has a future before her.

Dumby: Mrs. Erlynne has a past before her.

Lord Augustus: I prefer women with a past. They're always so demmed amusing to talk to.

Cecil Graham: Well, you'll have lots of topics of conversation with her, Tuppy. (*Rising and going to him.*)

Lord Augustus: You're getting annoying, dear boy; you're getting demmed annoying.

Cecil Graham (*puts his hands on his shoulders*): Now, Tuppy, you've lost your figure and you've lost your character. Don't lose your temper; you have only got one.

Lord Augustus: My dear boy, if I wasn't the most good-natured man in London –

Cecil Graham: We'd treat you with more respect, wouldn't we, Tuppy? (*Strolls away.*)

Dumby: The youth of the present day are quite monstrous. They have absolutely no respect for dyed hair.

LORD AUGUSTUS *looks round angrily.*

Cecil Graham: Mrs. Erlynne has a very great respect for dear Tuppy.

Dumby: Then Mrs. Erlynne sets an admirable example to the rest of her sex. It is perfectly brutal the way most women nowadays behave to men who are not their husbands.

Lord Windermere: Dumby, you are ridiculous, and Cecil, you let your tongue run away with you. You must leave Mrs. Erlynne alone. You don't really know anything about her, and you're always talking scandal against her.

Cecil Graham (*coming towards him L.C.*): My dear Arthur, I never talk scandal. I only talk gossip.

Lord Windermere: What is the difference between scandal and gossip?

Cecil Graham: Oh! gossip is charming! History is merely gossip. But scandal is gossip made tedious by morality. Now, I never moralise. A man who moralises is usually a hypocrite, and a woman who moralises is invariably plain. There is nothing in the whole world so unbecoming to a woman as a Nonconformist conscience. And most women know it, I'm glad to say.

Lord Augustus: Just my sentiments, dear boy, just my sentiments.

Cecil Graham: Sorry to hear it, Tuppy; whenever people agree with me, I always feel I must be wrong.

Lord Augustus: My dear boy, when I was your age –

Cecil Graham: But you never were, Tuppy, and you never will be. (*Goes up C.*) I say, Darlington, let us have some cards. You'll play, Arthur, won't you?

Lord Windermere: No, thanks, Cecil.

Dumby (*with a sigh*): Good heavens! how marriage ruins a man! It's as demoralising as cigarettes, and far more expensive.

Cecil Graham: You'll play, of course, Tuppy?

Lord Augustus (*pouring himself out a brandy and soda at table*): Can't, dear boy. Promised Mrs. Erlynne never to play or drink again.

Cecil Graham: Now, my dear Tuppy, don't be led astray into the paths of virtue. Reformed, you would be perfectly tedious. That is the worst of women. They always want one to be good. And if we are good, when they meet us, they don't love us at all. They like to find us quite irretrievably bad, and to leave us quite unattractively good.

Lord Darlington (*rising from R. table, where he has been writing letters*): They always do find us bad!

Dumby: I don't think we are bad. I think we are all good, except Tuppy.

Lord Darlington: No, we are all in the gutter, but some of us are looking at the stars. (*Sits down at C. table.*)

Dumby: We are all in the gutter, but some of us are looking at the stars? Upon my word, you are very romantic to-night, Darlington.

Cecil Graham: Too romantic! You must be in love. Who is the girl?

Lord Darlington: The woman I love is not free, or thinks she isn't. (*Glances instinctively at* LORD WINDERMERE *while he speaks.*)

Cecil Graham: A married woman, then! Well, there's nothing in the world like the devotion of a married woman. It's a thing no married man knows anything about.

Lord Darlington: Oh! she doesn't love me. She is a good woman. She is the only good woman I have ever met in my life.

Cecil Graham: The only good woman you have ever met in your life?

Lord Darlington: Yes!

Cecil Graham (*lighting a cigarette*): Well, you are a lucky fellow! Why, I have met hundreds of good women. I never seem to meet any but good women. The world is perfectly packed with good women. To know them is a middle-class education.

Lord Darlington: This woman has purity and innocence. She has everything we men have lost.

Cecil Graham: My dear fellow, what on earth should we men do going about with purity and innocence? A carefully thought-out buttonhole is much more effective.

Dumby: She doesn't really love you then?

Lord Darlington: No, she does not!

Dumby: I congratulate you, my dear fellow. In this world there are only two tragedies. One is not getting what one wants, and the other is getting it. The last is much the worst; the last is a real tragedy! But I am interested to hear she does not love you. How long could you love a woman who didn't love you, Cecil?

Cecil Graham: A woman who didn't love me? Oh, all my life!

Dumby: So could I. But it's so difficult to meet one.

Lord Darlington: How can you be so conceited, Dumby?

Dumby: I didn't say it as a matter of conceit. I said it as a matter of regret. I have been wildly, madly adored. I am sorry I have. It has been an immense nuisance. I should like to be allowed a little time to myself now and then.

Lord Augustus (looking round): Time to educate yourself, I suppose.

Dumby: No, time to forget all I have learned. That is much more important, dear Tuppy.

LORD AUGUSTUS *moves uneasily in his chair.*

Lord Darlington: What cynics you fellows are!

Cecil Graham: What is a cynic? (*Sitting on the back of the sofa.*)

Lord Darlington: A man who knows the price of everything and the value of nothing.

Cecil Graham: And a sentimentalist, my dear Darlington, is a man who sees an absurd value in everything, and doesn't know the market price of any single thing.

Lord Darlington: You always amuse me, Cecil. You talk as if you were a man of experience.

Cecil Graham: I am. (*Moves to front of fireplace.*)

Lord Darlington: You are far too young!

Cecil Graham: That is a great error. Experience is a question of instinct about life. I have got it. Tuppy hasn't. Experience is the name Tuppy gives to his mistakes. That is all.

LORD AUGUSTUS *looks round indignantly.*

Dumby: Experience is the name every one gives to their mistakes.

Cecil Graham (standing with his back to the fireplace): One shouldn't commit any. (*Sees* LADY WINDERMERE'S *fan on sofa.*)

Dumby: Life would be very dull without them.

Cecil Graham: Of course you are quite faithful to this woman you are in love with, Darlington, to this good woman?

Lord Darlington: Cecil, if one really loves a woman, all other women in the world become absolutely meaningless to one. Love changes one – I am changed.

Cecil Graham: Dear me! How very interesting! Tuppy, I want to talk to you.

LORD AUGUSTUS *takes no notice.*

Dumby: It's no use talking to Tuppy. You might just as well talk to a brick wall.

Cecil Graham: But I like talking to a brick wall – it's the only thing in the world that never contradicts me! Tuppy!

Lord Augustus: Well, what is it? What is it? (*Rising and going over to* CECIL GRAHAM.)

Cecil Graham: Come over here. I want you particularly. (*Aside.*) Darlington has been moralising and talking about the purity of love, and that sort of thing, and he has got some woman in his rooms all the time.

Lord Augustus: No, really! really!

Cecil Graham (in a low voice): Yes, here is her fan. (*Points to the fan.*)

Lord Augustus (chuckling): By Jove! By Jove!

Lord Windermere (up by door): I am really off now, Lord Darlington. I am sorry you are leaving England so soon. Pray call on us when you come back! My wife and I will be charmed to see you!

Lord Darlington (up stage with LORD WINDERMERE*):* I am afraid I shall be away for many years. Goodnight!

Cecil Graham: Arthur!

Lord Windermere: What?

Cecil Graham: I want to speak to you for a moment. No, do come!

Lord Windermere (putting on his coat): I can't – I'm off.

Cecil Graham: It is something very particular. It will interest you enormously.

Lord Windermere (smiling): It is some of your nonsense, Cecil.

Cecil Graham: It isn't! It isn't really.

Lord Augustus (going to him): My dear fellow, you mustn't go yet. I have a lot to talk to you about. And Cecil has something to show you.

Lord Windermere (walking over): Well, what is it?

Cecil Graham: Darlington has got a woman here in his rooms. Here is her fan. Amusing, isn't it? (*A pause.*)

Lord Windermere: Good God! (*Seizes the fan* – DUMBY *rises.*)

Cecil Graham: What is the matter?

Lord Windermere: Lord Darlington!

Lord Darlington (turning round): Yes!

Lord Windermere: What is my wife's fan doing here in your rooms? Hands off, Cecil. Don't touch me.

Lord Darlington: Your wife's fan?

Lord Windermere: Yes, here it is.

Lord Darlington (walking towards him): I don't know!

Lord Windermere: You must know. I demand an explanation. Don't hold me, you fool. (*To* CECIL GRAHAM.)

Lord Darlington (aside): She is here after all!

Lord Windermere: Speak, sir! Why is my wife's fan here? Answer me! By God! I'll search your rooms, and if my wife's here, I'll – (*Moves.*)

Lord Darlington: You shall not search my rooms. You have no right to do so. I forbid you!

Lord Windermere: You scoundrel! I'll not leave your room till I have searched every corner of it! What moves behind that curtain? (*Rushes towards the curtain C.*)

Mrs. Erlynne (enters behind R.): Lord Windermere!

Lord Windermere: Mrs. Erlynne!

Every one starts and turns round. LADY WINDERMERE *slides out from behind the curtain and glides from the room L.*

Mrs. Erlynne: I am afraid I took your wife's fan in mistake for my own, when I was leaving your house to-night. I am so sorry. (*Takes fan from him.* LORD WINDERMERE *looks at her in contempt.* LORD DARLINGTON *in mingled astonishment and anger.* LORD AUGUSTUS *turns away. The other men smile at each other.*)

ACT DROP.

FOURTH ACT

SCENE

Same as in Act I.

Lady Windermere (lying on sofa): How can I tell him? I can't tell him. It would kill me. I wonder what happened after I escaped from that horrible room. Perhaps she told them the true reason of her being there, and the real meaning of that – fatal fan of mine. Oh, if he knows – how can I look him in the face again? He would never forgive me. (*Touches bell.*) How securely one thinks one lives out of reach of temptation, sin, folly. And then suddenly – Oh! Life is terrible. It rules us, we do not rule it.

Enter ROSALIE R.

Rosalie: Did your ladyship ring for me?

Lady Windermere: Yes. Have you found out at what time Lord Windermere came in last night?

Rosalie: His lordship did not come in till five o'clock.

Lady Windermere: Five o'clock? He knocked at my door this morning, didn't he?

Rosalie: Yes, my lady – at half-past nine. I told him your ladyship was not awake yet.

Lady Windermere: Did he say anything?

Rosalie: Something about your ladyship's fan. I didn't quite catch what his lordship said. Has the fan been lost, my lady? I can't find it, and Parker says it was not left in any of the rooms. He has looked in all of them and on the terrace as well.

Lady Windermere: It doesn't matter. Tell Parker not to trouble. That will do.

Exit Rosalie.

Lady Windermere (rising): She is sure to tell him. I can fancy a person doing a wonderful act of self-sacrifice, doing it spontaneously, recklessly, nobly – and afterwards finding out that it costs too much. Why should she hesitate between her ruin and mine? . . . How strange! I would have publicly disgraced her in my own house. She accepts public disgrace in the house of another to save me. . . . There is a bitter irony in things, a bitter irony in the way we talk of good and bad women. . . . Oh, what a lesson! and what a pity that in life we only get our lessons when they are of no use to us! For even if she doesn't tell, I must. Oh! the shame of it, the shame of it. To tell it is to live through it all again. Actions are the first tragedy in life, words are the second. Words are perhaps the worst. Words are merciless. . . . Oh! (*Starts as* LORD WINDER-MERE *enters.*)

Lord Windermere (*kisses her*): Margaret – how pale you look!

Lady Windermere: I slept very badly.

Lord Windermere (*sitting on sofa with her*): I am so sorry. I came in dreadfully late, and didn't like to wake you. You are crying, dear.

Lady Windermere: Yes, I am crying, for I have something to tell you, Arthur.

Lord Windermere: My dear child, you are not well. You've been doing too much. Let us go away to the country. You'll be all right at Selby. The season is almost over. There is no use staying on. Poor darling! We'll go away to-day, if you like. (*Rises.*) We can easily catch the 3.40. I'll send a wire to Fannen. (*Crosses and sits down at table to write a telegram.*)

Lady Windermere: Yes; let us go away to-day. No; I can't go to-day, Arthur. There is some one I must see before I leave town – some one who has been kind to me.

Lord Windermere (*rising and leaning over sofa*): Kind to you?

Lady Windermere: Far more than that. (*Rises and goes to him.*) I will tell you, Arthur, but only love me, love me as you used to love me.

Lord Windermere: Used to? You are not thinking of that wretched woman who came here last night? (*Coming round and sitting R. of her*): You don't still imagine – no, you couldn't.

Lady Windermere: I don't. I know now I was wrong and foolish.

Lord Windermere: It was very good of you to receive her last night – but you are never to see her again.

Lady Windermere: Why do you say that? (*A pause.*)

Lord Windermere (*holding her hand*): Margaret, I thought Mrs. Erlynne was a woman more sinned against than sinning, as the phrase goes. I thought she wanted to be good, to get back into a place that she had lost by a moment's folly, to lead again a decent life. I believed what she told me – I was mistaken in her. She is bad – as bad as a woman can be.

Lady Windermere: Arthur, Arthur, don't talk so bitterly about any woman. I don't think now that people can be divided into the good and the bad as though they were two separate races or creations. What are called good women may have terrible things in them, mad moods of recklessness, assertion, jealousy, sin. Bad women, as they are termed, may have in them sorrow, repentance, pity, sacrifice. And I don't think Mrs. Erlynne a bad woman – I know she's not.

Lord Windermere: My dear child, the woman's impossible. No matter what harm she tries to do us, you must never see her again. She is inadmissible anywhere.

Lady Windermere: But I want to see her. I want her to come here.

Lord Windermere: Never!

Lady Windermere: She came here once as *your* guest. She must come now as *mine*. That is but fair.

Lord Windermere: She should never have come here.

Lady Windermere (rising): It is too late, Arthur, to say that now. (*Moves away.*)

Lord Windermere (rising): Margaret, if you knew where Mrs. Erlynne went last night, after she left this house, you would not sit in the same room with her. It was absolutely shameless, the whole thing.

Lady Windermere: Arthur, I can't bear it any longer. I must tell you. Last night –

Enter PARKER *with a tray on which lie* LADY WINDER-MERE'S *fan and a card.*

Parker: Mrs. Erlynne has called to return your ladyship's fan which she took away by mistake last night. Mrs. Erlynne has written a message on the card.

Lady Windermere: Oh, ask Mrs. Erlynne to be kind enough to come up. (*Reads card.*) Say I shall be very glad to see her.

Exit PARKER.

She wants to see me, Arthur.

Lord Windermere (takes card and looks at it): Margaret, I beg you not to. Let me see her first, at any rate. She's a dangerous woman. She is the most dangerous woman I know. You don't realise what you're doing.

Lady Windermere: It is right that I should see her.

Lord Windermere: My child, you may be on the brink of a great sorrow. Don't go to meet it. It is absolutely necessary that I should see her before you do.

Lady Windermere: Why should it be necessary?

Enter PARKER.

Parker: Mrs. Erlynne.

Enter MRS. ERLYNNE. *Exit* PARKER.

Mrs. Erlynne: How do you do, Lady Windermere? (*To* LORD WINDERMERE.) How do you do? Do you know, Lady Windermere, I am so sorry about your fan. I can't imagine how I made such a silly mistake. Most stupid of me. And as I was driving in your direction, I thought I would take the opportunity of returning your property in person with many apologies for my carelessness, and of bidding you good-bye.

Lady Windermere: Good-bye? (*Moves towards sofa with* MRS. ERLYNNE *and sits down beside her*.) Are you going away, then, Mrs. Erlynne?

Mrs. Erlynne: Yes; I am going to live abroad again. The English climate doesn't suit me. My – heart is affected here, and that I don't like. I prefer living in the south. London is too full of fogs and – and serious people, Lord Windermere. Whether the fogs produce the serious people or whether the serious people produce the fogs, I don't know, but the whole thing rather gets on my nerves, and so I'm leaving this afternoon by the Club Train.

Lady Windermere: This afternoon? But I wanted so much to come and see you.

Mrs. Erlynne: How kind of you! But I am afraid I have to go.

Lady Windermere: Shall I never see you again, Mrs. Erlynne?

Mrs. Erlynne: I am afraid not. Our lives lie too far apart. But there is a little thing I would like you to do for me. I want a photograph of you, Lady Windermere – would you give me one? You don't know how gratified I should be.

Lady Windermere: Oh, with pleasure. There is one on that table. I'll show it to you. (*Goes across to the table*.)

Lord Windermere (*coming up to* MRS. ERLYNNE *and speaking in a low voice*): It is monstrous your intruding yourself here after your conduct last night.

Mrs. Erlynne (*with an amused smile*): My dear Windermere, manners before morals!

Lady Windermere (*returning*): I'm afraid it is very flattering – I am not so pretty as that. (*Showing photograph*.)

Mrs. Erlynne: You are much prettier. But haven't you got one of yourself with your little boy?

Lady Windermere: I have. Would you prefer one of those?

Mrs. Erlynne: Yes.

Lady Windermere: I'll go and get it for you, if you'll excuse me for a moment. I have one upstairs.

Mrs. Erlynne: So sorry, Lady Windermere, to give you so much trouble.

Lady Windermere (*moves to door R.*): No trouble at all, Mrs. Erlynne.

Mrs. Erlynne: Thanks so much.

Exit LADY WINDERMERE *R.*

You seem rather out of temper this morning, Windermere. Why should you be? Margaret and I get on charmingly together.

Lord Windermere: I can't bear to see you with her. Besides, you have not told me the truth, Mrs. Erlynne.

Mrs Erlynne: I have not told *her* the truth, you mean.

Lord Windermere (*standing C.*): I sometimes wish you had. I should have been spared then the misery, the anxiety, the annoyance of the last six months. But rather than my wife should know – that the mother whom she was taught to consider as dead, the mother whom she has mourned as dead, is living – a divorced woman, going about under an assumed name, a bad woman preying upon life, as I know you now to be – rather than that, I was ready to supply you with money to pay bill after bill, extravagance after extravagance, to risk what occurred yesterday, the first quarrel I have ever had with my wife. You don't understand what that means to me. How could you? But I tell you that the only bitter words that ever came from those sweet lips of hers were on your account, and I hate to see you next her. You sully the innocence that is in her. (*Moves L.C.*) And then I used to think that with all your faults you were frank and honest. You are not.

Mrs. Erlynne: Why do you say that?

Lord Windermere: You made me get you an invitation to my wife's ball.

Mrs. Erlynne: For my daughter's ball – yes.

Lord Windermere: You came, and within an hour of your leaving the house you are found in a man's rooms – you are disgraced before every one. (*Goes up stage C.*)

Mrs. Erlynne: Yes.

Lord Windermere (*turning round on her*): Therefore I have a right to look upon you as what you are – a worthless, vicious woman. I have the right to tell you never to enter this house, never to attempt to come near my wife –

Mrs. Erlynne (*coldly*): My daughter, you mean.

Lord Windermere: You have no right to claim her as your daughter. You left her, abandoned her when she was but a child in the cradle, abandoned her for your lover, who abandoned you in turn.

Mrs. Erlynne (*rising*): Do you count that to his credit, Lord Windermere – or to mine?

Lord Windermere: To his, now that I know you.

Mrs. Erlynne: Take care – you had better be careful.

Lord Windermere: Oh, I am not going to mince words for you. I know you thoroughly.

Mrs. Erlynne (*looking steadily at him*): I question that.

Lord Windermere: I *do* know you. For twenty years of your life you lived without your child, without a thought of your child. One day you read in the papers that she had married a rich man. You saw your hideous chance. You knew that to spare her the ignominy of learning that a woman like you was her mother, I would endure anything. You began your blackmailing.

Mrs. Erlynne (*shrugging her shoulders*): Don't use ugly words, Windermere. They are vulgar. I saw my chance, it is true, and took it.

Lord Windermere: Yes, you took it – and spoiled it all last night by being found out.

Mrs. Erlynne (*with a strange smile*): You are quite right, I spoiled it all last night.

Lord Windermere: And as for your blunder in taking my wife's fan from here and then leaving it about in Darlington's rooms, it is unpardonable. I can't bear the sight of it now. I shall never let my wife use it again. The thing is soiled for me. You should have kept it and not brought it back.

Mrs. Erlynne: I think I *shall* keep it. (*Goes up.*) It's extremely pretty. (*Takes up fan.*) I shall ask Margaret to give it to me.

Lord Windermere: I hope my wife will give it you.

Mrs. Erlynne: Oh, I'm sure she will have no objection.

Lord Windermere: I wish that at the same time she would give you a miniature she kisses every night before she prays. – It's the miniature of a young innocent-looking girl with beautiful dark hair.

Mrs. Erlynne: Ah, yes, I remember. How long ago that seems! (*Goes to sofa and sits down.*) It was done before I was married. Dark hair and an innocent expression were the fashion then, Windermere! (*A pause.*)

Lord Windermere: What do you mean by coming here this morning? What is your object? (*Crossing L.C. and sitting.*)

Mrs. Erlynne (*with a note of irony in her voice*): To bid good-bye to my dear daughter, of course.

LORD WINDERMERE *bites his under lip in anger.* MRS. ERLYNNE *looks at him, and her voice and manner become serious. In her accents as she talks there is a note of deep tragedy. For a moment she reveals herself.*

Oh, don't imagine I am going to have a pathetic scene with her, weep on her neck and tell her who I am, and all that kind of thing. I have no ambition to play the part of a mother. Only once in my life have I known a mother's feelings. That was last night. They were terrible – they made me suffer – they made me suffer too much. For twenty years, as you say, I have lived childless – I want to live childless still. (*Hiding her feelings with a trivial laugh.*) Besides, my dear Windermere, how on earth could I pose as a mother with a grown-up daughter? Margaret is twenty-one, and I have never admitted that I am more than twenty-nine, or thirty at the most. Twenty-nine when there are pink shades, thirty when there are not. So you see what difficulties it would involve. No, as far as I am concerned, let your wife cherish the memory of this dead, stainless mother. Why should I interfere with her illusions? I find it hard enough to keep my own. I lost one illusion last night. I thought I had no heart. I find I have, and a heart doesn't suit me, Windermere. Somehow it doesn't go with modern dress. It makes one look old. (*Takes up hand-mirror from table and looks into it.*) And it spoils one's career at critical moments.

Lord Windermere: You fill me with horror – with absolute horror.

Mrs. Erlynne (*rising*): I suppose, Windermere, you would like me to retire into a convent, or become a hospital nurse, or something of that kind, as people do in silly modern novels. That is stupid of you, Arthur; in real life we don't do such things – not as long as we have any good looks left, at any rate. No – what consoles one nowadays is not repentance, but pleasure. Repentance is quite out of date. And besides, if a woman really repents, she has to go to a bad dressmaker, otherwise no one believes in her. And nothing in the world would induce me to do that. No; I am going to pass entirely out of your two lives. My coming into them has been a mistake – I discovered that last night.

Lord Windermere: A fatal mistake.

Mrs. Erlynne (smiling): Almost fatal.

Lord Windermere: I am sorry now I did not tell my wife the whole thing at once.

Mrs. Erlynne: I regret my bad actions. You regret your good ones – that is the difference between us.

Lord Windermere: I don't trust you. I *will* tell my wife. It's better for her to know, and from me. It will cause her infinite pain – it will humiliate her terribly, but it's right that she should know.

Mrs. Erlynne: You propose to tell her?

Lord Windermere: I am going to tell her.

Mrs. Erlynne (going up to him): If you do, I will make my name so infamous that it will mar every moment of her life. It will ruin her, and make her wretched. If you dare to tell her, there is no depth of degradation I will not sink to, no pit of shame I will not enter. You shall not tell her – I forbid you.

Lord Windermere: Why?

Mrs. Erlynne (after a pause): If I said to you that I cared for her, perhaps loved her even – you would sneer at me, wouldn't you?

Lord Windermere: I should feel it was not true. A mother's love means devotion, unselfishness, sacrifice. What could you know of such things?

Mrs. Erlynne: You are right. What could I know of such things? Don't let us talk any more about it – as for telling my daughter who I am, that I do not allow. It is my secret it is not yours. If I make up my mind to tell her, and I think I will, I shall tell her before I leave the house – if not, I shall never tell her.

Lord Windermere (angrily): Then let me beg of you to leave our house at once. I will make your excuses to Margaret.

Enter LADY WINDERMERE *R. She goes over to* MRS. ERLYNNE *with the photograph in her hand.* LORD WINDERMERE *moves to back of sofa, and anxiously watches* MRS. ERLYNNE *as the scene progresses.*

Lady Windermere: I am so sorry, Mrs. Erlynne, to have kept you waiting. I couldn't find the photograph anywhere. At last I discovered it in my husband's dressing-room – he had stolen it.

Mrs. Erlynne (takes the photograph from her and looks at it): I am not surprised – it is charming. *(Goes over to sofa with* LADY WINDER-

MERE, *and sits down beside her. Looks again at the photograph.*) And so that is your little boy! What is he called?

Lady Windermere: Gerard, after my dear father.

Mrs. Erlynne (laying the photograph down): Really?

Lady Windermere: Yes. If it had been a glrl, I would have called it after my mother. My mother had the same name as myself, Margaret.

Mrs. Erlynne: My name is Margaret too.

Lady Windermere: Indeed!

Mrs. Erlynne: Yes. (*Pause.*) You are devoted to your mother's memory, Lady Windermere, your husband tells me.

Lady Windermere: We all have ideals in life. At least we all should have. Mine is my mother.

Mrs. Erlynne: Ideals are dangerous things. Realities are better. They wound, but they're better.

Lady Windermere (shaking her head): If I lost my ideals, I should lose everything.

Mrs. Erlynne: Everything?

Lady Windermere: Yes. (*Pause.*)

Mrs. Erlynne: Did your father often speak to you of your mother?

Lady Windermere: No, it gave him too much pain. He told me how my mother had died a few months after I was born. His eyes filled with tears as he spoke. Then he begged me never to mention her name to him again. It made him suffer even to hear it. My father – my father really died of a broken heart. His was the most ruined life I know.

Mrs. Erlynne (rising): I am afraid I must go now, Lady Windermere.

Lady Windermere (rising): Oh no, don't.

Mrs. Erlynne: I think I had better. My carriage must have come back by this time. I sent it to Lady Jedburgh's with a note.

Lady Windermere: Arthur, would you mind seeing if Mrs. Erlynne's carriage has come back?

Mrs. Erlynne: Pray don't trouble, Lord Windermere.

Lady Windermere: Yes, Arthur, do go, please.

LORD WINDERMERE *hesitates for a moment and looks at* MRS. ERLYNNE. *She remains quite impassive. He leaves the room.*

(*To* MRS. ERLYNNE.) Oh! What am I to say to you? You saved me last night? (*Goes towards her.*)

Mrs. Erlynne: Hush – don't speak of it.

Lady Windermere: I must speak of it. I can't let you think that I am going to accept this sacrifice. I am not. It is too great. I am going to tell my husband everything. It is my duty.

Mrs. Erlynne: It is not your duty – at least you have duties to others besides him. You say you owe me something?

Lady Windermere: I owe you everything.

Mrs. Erlynne: Then pay your debt by silence. That is the only way in which it can be paid. Don't spoil the one good thing I have done in my life by telling it to any one. Promise me that what passed last night will remain a secret between us. You must not bring misery into your husband's life. Why spoil his love? You must not spoil it. Love is easily killed. Oh! how easily love is killed. Pledge me your word, Lady Windermere, that you will never tell him. I insist upon it.

Lady Windermere (with bowed head): It is your will, not mine.

Mrs. Erlynne: Yes, it is my will. And never forget your child – I like to think of you as a mother. I like you to think of yourself as one.

Lady Windermere (looking up): I always will now. Only once in my life I have forgotten my own mother – that was last night. Oh, if I had remembered her I should not have been so foolish, so wicked.

Mrs. Erlynne (with a slight shudder): Hush, last night is quite over.

Enter LORD WINDERMERE.

Lord Windermere: Your carriage has not come back yet, Mrs. Erlynne.

Mrs. Erlynne: It makes no matter. I'll take a hansom. There is nothing in the world so respectable as a good Shrewsbury and Talbot. And now, dear Lady Windermere, I am afraid it is really good-bye. (*Moves up C.*) Oh, I remember. You'll think me absurd, but do you know I've taken a great fancy to this fan that I was silly enough to run away with last night from your ball. Now, I wonder would you give it to me? Lord Windermere says you may. I know it is his present.

Lady Windermere: Oh, certainly, if it will give you any pleasure. But it has my name on it. It has 'Margaret' on it.

Mrs. Erlynne: But we have the same Christian name.

Lady Windermere: Oh, I forgot. Of course, do have it. What a wonderful chance our names being the same!

Mrs. Erlynne: Quite wonderful. Thanks – it will always remind me of you. (*Shakes hands with her.*)

Enter PARKER.

Parker: Lord Augustus Lorton. Mrs. Erlynne's carriage has come.

Enter LORD AUGUSTUS.

Lord Augustus: Good-morning, dear boy. Good-morning, Lady Windermere. (*Sees* MRS. ERLYNNE.) Mrs. Erlynne!

Mrs. Erlynne: How do you do, Lord Augustus? Are you quite well this morning?

Lord Augustus (coldly): Quite well, thank you, Mrs. Erlynne.

Mrs. Erlynne: You don't look at all well, Lord Augustus. You stop up too late – it is so bad for you. You really should take more care of yourself. Goodbye, Lord Windermere. (*Goes towards door with a bow to* LORD AUGUSTUS. *Suddenly smiles and looks back at him.*) Lord Augustus! Won't you see me to my carriage? You might carry the fan.

Lord Windermere: Allow me!

Mrs. Erlynne: No; I want Lord Augustus. I have a special message for the dear Duchess. Won't you carry the fan, Lord Augustus?

Lord Augustus: If you really desire it, Mrs. Erlynne.

Mrs. Erlynne (laughing): Of course I do. You'll carry it so gracefully. You would carry off anything gracefully, dear Lord Augustus. (*When she reaches the door she looks back for a moment at* LADY WINDERMERE. *Their eyes meet. Then she turns, and exit C. followed by* LORD AUGUSTUS.)

Lady Windermere: You will never speak against Mrs. Erlynne again, Arthur, will you?

Lord Windermere (gravely): She is better than one thought her.

Lady Windermere: She is better than I am.

Lord Windermere (smiling as he strokes her hair): Child, you and she belong to different worlds. Into your world evil has never entered.

Lady Windermere: Don't say that, Arthur. There is the same world for all of us, and good and evil, sin and innocence, go through it hand in hand. To shut one's eyes to half of life that one may live securely is as though one blinded oneself that one might walk with more safety in a land of pit and precipice.

Lord Windermere (moves down with her): Darling, why do you say that?

Lady Windermere (sits on sofa): Because I, who had shut my eyes to life, came to the brink. And one who had separated us –

Lord Windermere: We were never separated.

Lady Windermere: We never must be again. Oh Arthur, don't love me less, and I will trust you more. I will trust you absolutely. Let us go to Selby. In the Rose Garden at Selby the roses are white and red.

Enter LORD AUGUSTUS *C.*

Lord Augustus: Arthur, she has explained everything!

LADY WINDERMERE *looks horribly frightened at this.* LORD WINDERMERE *starts.* LORD AUGUSTUS *takes* WINDERMERE *by the arm and brings him to front of stage. He talks rapidly and in a low voice.* LADY WINDERMERE *stands watching them in terror.*

My dear fellow, she has explained every demmed thing. We all wronged her immensely. It was entirely for my sake she went to Darlington's rooms. Called first at the Club – fact is, wanted to put me out of suspense – and being told I had gone on – followed – naturally frightened when she heard a lot of us coming in – retired to another room – I assure you, most gratifying to me, the whole thing. We all behaved brutally to her. She is just the woman for me. Suits me down to the ground. All the conditions she makes are that we live entirely out of England. A very good thing too. Demmed clubs, demmed climate, demmed cooks, demmed everything. Sick of it all!

Lady Windermere (frightened): Has Mrs. Erlynne – ?

Lord Augustus (advancing towards her with a low bow): Yes, Lady Windermere – Mrs. Erlynne has done me the honour of accepting my hand.

Lord Windermere: Well, you are certainly marrying a very clever woman!

Lady Windermere (taking her husband's hand): Ah, you're marrying a very good woman!

CURTAIN.

A WOMAN OF NO IMPORTANCE

THE PERSONS OF THE PLAY

LORD ILLINGWORTH
SIR JOHN PONTEFRACT
LORD ALFRED RUFFORD
MR. KELVIL, M.P.
THE VEN. ARCHDEACON DAUBENY, D. D.
GERALD ARBUTHNOT
FARQUHAR, Butler
FRANCIS, Footman

LADY HUNSTANTON
LADY CAROLINE PONTEFRACT
LADY STUTFIELD
MRS. ALLONBY
MISS HESTER WORSLEY
ALICE, Maid
MRS. ARBUTHNOT

THE SCENES OF THE PLAY

ACT I. *The terrace at Hunstanton Chase.*
ACT II. *The drawing-room at Hunstanton Chase.*
ACT III. *The Hall at Hunstanton Chase.*
ACT IV. *Sitting-room in Mrs. Arbuthnot's house at Wrockley.*
TIME: *The Present.*
PLACE: *The Shires.*

The action of the play takes place within twenty-four hours.

LONDON: HAYMARKET THEATRE

Lessee and Manager: Mr. H. Beerbohm Tree
April 19th, 1893

LORD ILLINGWORTH	*Mr. Tree*
SIR JOHN PONTEFRACT	*Mr. E. Holman Clark*
LORD ALFRED RUFFORD	*Mr. Ernest Lawford*
MR. KELVIL, M.P.	*Mr. Charles Allan*
THE VEN. ARCHDEACON	
DAUBENY, D.D.	*Mr. Kemble*
GERALD ARBUTHNOT	*Mr. Terry*
FARQUHAR (Butler)	*Mr. Hay*
FRANCIS (Footman)	*Mr. Montague*
LADY HUNSTANTON	*Miss Rose Leclercq*
LADY CAROLINE PONTEFRACT	*Miss Le Thèire*
LADY STUTFIELD	*Miss Blanche Horlock*
MRS. ALLONBY	*Mrs. Tree*
MISS HESTER WORSLEY	*Miss Julia Neilson*
ALICE (Maid)	*Miss Kelly*
MRS ARBUTHNOT	*Mrs. Bernard-Beere*

FIRST ACT

SCENE

Lawn in front of the terrace at Hunstanton.

SIR JOHN *and* LADY CAROLINE PONTEFRACT, MISS
WORSLEY, *on chairs under large yew tree.*

Lady Caroline: I believe this is the first English country house you
have stayed at, Miss Worsley?

Hester: Yes, Lady Caroline.

Lady Caroline: You have no country houses, I am told, in America?

Hester: We have not many.

Lady Caroline: Have you any country? What we should call country?

Hester (smiling): We have the largest country in the world, Lady
Caroline. They used to tell us at school that some of our states are
as big as France and England put together.

Lady Caroline: Ah! you must find it very draughty, I should fancy.
(*To* SIR JOHN.) John, you should have your muffler. What is the
use of my always knitting mufflers for you if you won't wear them?

Sir John: I am quite warm, Caroline, I assure you.

Lady Caroline: I think not, John. Well, you couldn't come to a
more charming place than this, Miss Worsley, though the house is
excessively damp, quite unpardonably damp, and dear Lady Hunstanton is sometimes a little lax about the people she asks down
here. (*To* SIR JOHN.) Jane mixes too much. Lord Illingworth, of
course, is a man of high distinction. It is a privilege to meet him.
And that member of Parliament, Mr. Kettle –

Sir John: Kelvil, my love, Kelvil.

Lady Caroline: He must be quite respectable. One has never heard
his name before in the whole course of one's life, which speaks vol-
umes for a man, nowadays. But Mrs. Allonby is hardly a very suitable person.

Hester: I dislike Mrs. Allonby. I dislike her more than I can say.

Lady Caroline: I am not sure, Miss Worsley, that foreigners like

yourself should cultivate likes or dislikes about the people they are
invited to meet. Mrs. Allonby is very well born. She is a niece of
Lord Brancaster's. It is said, of course, that she ran away twice
before she was married. But you know how unfair people often are.
I myself don't believe she ran away more than once.

Hester: Mr. Arbuthnot is very charming.

Lady Caroline: Ah, yes! the young man who has a post in a bank.
Lady Hunstanton is most kind in asking him here, and Lord Illingworth seems to have taken quite a fancy to him. I am not sure, however, that Jane is right in taking him out of his position. In my
young days, Miss Worsley, one never met any one in society who
worked for their living. It was not considered the thing.

Hester: In America those are the people we respect most.

Lady Caroline: I have no doubt of it.

Hester: Mr. Arbuthnot has a beautiful nature! He is so simple, so
sincere. He has one of the most beautiful natures I have ever come
across. It is a privilege to meet *him*.

Lady Caroline: It is not customary in England, Miss Worsley, for a
young lady to speak with such enthusiasm of any person of the
opposite sex. English women conceal their feelings till after they are
married. They show them then.

Hester: Do you, in England, allow no friendship to exist between
a young man and a young girl?

Enter LADY HUNSTANTON, *followed by* FOOTMAN *with
shawls and a cushion.*

Lady Caroline: We think it very inadvisable. Jane, I was just saying
what a pleasant party you have asked us to meet. You have a wonderful power of selection. It is quite a gift.

Lady Hunstanton: Dear Caroline, how kind of you! I think we all
do fit in very nicely together. And I hope our charming American
visitor will carry back pleasant recollections of our English country
life. (*To Footman.*) The cushion, there, Francis. And my shawl. The
Shetland. Get the Shetland.

Exit Footman for shawl.

Enter GERALD ARBUTHNOT.

Gerald: Lady Hunstanton, I have such good news to tell you.
Lord Illingworth has just offered to make me his secretary.

Lady Hunstanton: His secretary? That is good news indeed, Gerald. It means a very brilliant future in store for you. Your dear mother will be delighted. I really must try and induce her to come up here to-night. Do you think she would, Gerald? I know how difficult it is to get her to go anywhere.

Gerald: Oh! I am sure she would, Lady Hunstanton, if she knew Lord Illingworth had made me such an offer.

Enter Footman with shawl.

Lady Hunstanton: I will write and tell her about it and ask her to come up and meet him. (*To Footman.*) Just wait, Francis. (*Writes letter.*)

Lady Caroline: That is a very wonderful opening for so young a man as you are, Mr. Arbuthnot.

Gerald: It is indeed, Lady Caroline. I trust I shall be able to show myself worthy of it.

Lady Caroline: I trust so.

Gerald (*to* HESTER): *You* have not congratulated me yet, Miss Worsley.

Hester: Are you very pleased about it?

Gerald: Of course I am. It means everything to me – things that were out of the reach of hope before may be within hope's reach now.

Hester: Nothing should be out of the reach of hope. Life is a hope.

Lady Hunstanton: I fancy, Caroline, that Diplomacy is what Lord Illingworth is aiming at. I heard that he was offered Vienna. But that may not be true.

Lady Caroline: I don't think that England should be represented abroad by an unmarried man, Jane. It might lead to complications.

Lady Hunstanton: You are too nervous, Caroline. Believe me, you are too nervous. Besides, Lord Illingworth may marry any day. I was in hopes he would have married Lady Kelso. But I believe he said her family was too large. Or was it her feet? I forget which. I regret it very much. She was made to be an ambassador's wife.

Lady Caroline: She certainly has a wonderful faculty of remembering people's names, and forgetting their faces.

Lady Hunstanton: Well, that is very natural, Caroline, is it not? (*To Footman.*) Tell Henry to wait for an answer. I have written a line to your dear mother, Gerald, to tell her your good news, and to say she really must come to dinner.

Exit Footman.

Gerald: That is awfully kind of you, Lady Hunstanton. (*To* HESTER.) Will you come for a stroll, Miss Worsley?

Hester: With pleasure. (*Exit with* GERALD.)

Lady Hunstanton: I am very much gratified at Gerald Arbuthnot's good fortune. He is quite a *protégé* of mine. And I am particularly pleased that Lord Illingworth should have made the offer of his own accord without my suggesting anything. Nobody likes to be asked favours. I remember poor Charlotte Pagden making herself quite unpopular one season, because she had a French governess she wanted to recommend to every one.

Lady Caroline: I saw the governess, Jane. Lady Pagden sent her to me. It was before Eleanor came out. She was far too good-looking to be in any respectable household. I don't wonder Lady Pagden was so anxious to get rid of her.

Lady Hunstanton: Ah, that explains it.

Lady Caroline: John, the grass is too damp for you. You had better go and put on your overshoes at once.

Sir John: I am quite comfortable, Caroline, I assure you.

Lady Caroline: You must allow me to be the best judge of that, John. Pray do as I tell you.

SIR JOHN *gets up and goes off.*

Lady Hunstanton: You spoil him, Caroline, you do indeed!

Enter MRS ALLONBY *and* LADY STUTFIELD

(*To* MRS ALLONBY.) Well, dear, I hope you like the park. It is said to be well timbered.

Mrs. Allonby: The trees are wonderful, Lady Hunstanton.

Lady Stutfield: Quite, quite wonderful.

Mrs. Allonby: But somehow, I feel sure that if I lived in the country for six months, I should become so unsophisticated that no one would take the slightest notice of me.

Lady Hunstanton: l assure you, dear, that the country has not that effect at all. Why, it was from Melthorpe, which is only two miles from here, that Lady Belton eloped with Lord Fethersdale. I remember the occurrence perfectly. Poor Lord Belton died three days afterwards of joy, or gout. I forget which. We had a large party staying here at the time so we were all very much interested in the whole affair.

Mrs. Allonby: I think to elope is cowardly. It's running away from danger. And danger has become so rare in modern life.

Lady Caroline: As far as I can make out, the young women of the present day seem to make it the sole object of their lives to be always playing with fire.

Mrs. Allonby: The one advantage of playing with fire, Lady Caroline, is that one never gets even singed. It is the people who don't know how to play with it who get burned up.

Lady Stutfield: Yes; I see that. It is very, very helpful.

Lady Hunstanton: I don't know how the world would get on with such a theory as that, dear Mrs. Allonby.

Lady Stutfield: Ah! The world was made for men and not for women.

Mrs. Allonby: Oh, don't say that, Lady Stutfield. We have a much better time than they have. There are far more things forbidden to us than are forbidden to them.

Lady Stutfield: Yes; that is quite, quite true. I had not thought of that.

Enter SIR JOHN *and* MR. KELVIL.

Lady Hunstanton: Well, Mr. Kelvil, have you got through your work?

Kelvil: I have finished my writing for the day, Lady Hunstanton. It has been an arduous task. The demands on the time of a public man are very heavy nowadays, very heavy indeed. And I don't think they meet with adequate recognition.

Lady Caroline: John, have you got your overshoes on?

Sir John: Yes, my love.

Lady Caroline: I think you had better come over here, John. It is more sheltered.

Sir John: I am quite comfortable, Caroline.

Lady Caroline: I think not, John. You had better sit beside me.

SIR JOHN *rises and goes across.*

Lady Stutfield: And what have you been writing about this morning, Mr. Kelvil?

Kelvil: On the usual subject, Lady Stutfield. On Purity.

Lady Stutfield: That must be such a very, very interesting thing to write about.

Kelvil: It is the one subject of really national importance, nowadays, Lady Stutfield. I purpose addressing my constituents on the question before Parliament meets. I find that the poorer classes of this country display a marked desire for a higher ethical standard.

Lady Stutfield: How quite, quite nice of them.

Lady Caroline: Are you in favour of women taking part in politics, Mr. Kettle?

Sir John: Kelvil, my love, Kelvil.

Kelvil: The growing influence of women is the one reassuring thing in our political life, Lady Caroline. Women are always on the side of morality, public and private.

Lady Stutfield: It is so very, very gratifying to hear you say that.

Lady Hunstanton: Ah, yes! – the moral qualities in women – that is the important thing. I am afraid, Caroline, that dear Lord Illingworth doesn't value the moral qualities in women as much as he should.

Enter LORD ILLINGWORTH.

Lady Stutfield: The world says that Lord Illingworth is very, very wicked.

Lord Illingworth: But what world says that, Lady Stutfield? It must be the next world. This world and I are on excellent terms. (*Sits down beside* MRS. ALLONBY.)

Lady Stutfield: Every one I know says you are very, very wicked.

Lord Illingworth: It is perfectly monstrous the way people go about, nowadays, saying things against one behind one's back that are absolutely and entirely true.

Lady Hunstanton: Dear Lord Illingworth is quite hopeless, Lady Stutfield. I have given up trying to reform him. It would take a Public Company with a Board of Directors and a paid Secretary to do that. But you have the secretary already, Lord Illingworth, haven't you? Gerald Arbuthnot has told us of his good fortune; it is really most kind of you.

Lord Illingworth: Oh, don't say that, Lady Hunstanton. Kind is a dreadful word. I took a great fancy to young Arbuthnot the moment I met him, and he'll be of considerable use to me in something I am foolish enough to think of doing.

Lady Hunstanton: He is an admirable young man. And his mother is one of my dearest friends. He has just gone for a walk with our pretty American. She is very pretty, is she not?

Lady Caroline: Far too pretty. These American girls carry off all the good matches. Why can't they stay in their own country? They are always telling us it is the Paradise of women.

Lord Illingworth: It is, Lady Caroline. That is why, like Eve, they are so extremely anxious to get out of it.

Lady Caroline: Who are Miss Worsley's parents?

Lord Illingworth: American women are wonderfully clever in concealing their parents.

Lady Hunstanton: My dear Lord Illingworth, what do you mean? Miss Worsley, Caroline, is an orphan. Her father was a very wealthy millionaire or philanthropist, or both, I believe, who entertained my son quite hospitably, when he visited Boston. I don't know how he made his money, originally.

Kelvil: I fancy in American dry goods.

Lady Hunstanton: What are American dry goods?

Lord Illingworth: American novels.

Lady Hunstanton: How very singular! . . . Well, from whatever source her large fortune came, I have a great esteem for Miss Worsley. She dresses exceedingly well. All Americans do dress well. They get their clothes in Paris.

Mrs. Allonby: They say, Lady Hunstanton, that when good Americans die they go to Paris.

Lady Hunstanton: Indeed? And when bad Americans die, where do they go to?

Lord Illingworth: Oh, they go to America.

Kelvil: I am afraid you don't appreciate America, Lord Illingworth. It is a very remarkable country, especially considering its youth.

Lord Illingworth: The youth of America is their oldest tradition. It has been going on now for three hundred years. To hear them talk one would imagine they were in their first childhood. As far as civilisation goes they are in their second.

Kelvil: There is undoubtedly a great deal of corruption in American politics. I suppose you allude to that?

Lord Illingworth: I wonder.

Lady Hunstanton: Politics are in a sad way everywhere, I am told. They certainly are in England. Dear Mr. Cardew is ruining the country. I wonder Mrs. Cardew allows him. I am sure, Lord Illingworth, you don't think that uneducated people should be allowed to have votes?

Lord Illingworth: I think they are the only people who should.

Kelvil: Do you take no side then in modern politics, Lord Illingworth?

Lord Illingworth: One should never take sides in anything, Mr. Kelvil. Taking sides is the beginning of sincerity, and earnestness follows shortly afterwards and the human being becomes a bore. However, the House of Commons really does very little harm. You can't make people good by Act of Parliament – that is something.

Kelvil: You cannot deny that the House of Commons has always shown great sympathy with the sufferings of the poor.

Lord Illingworth: That is its special vice. That is the special vice of the age. One should sympathise with the joy, the beauty, the colour of life. The less said about life's sores the better, Mr. Kelvil.

Kelvil: Still our East End is a very important problem.

Lord Illingworth: Quite so. It is the problem of slavery. And we are trying to solve it by amusing the slaves.

Lady Hunstanton: Certainly, a great deal may be done by means of cheap entertainments, as you say, Lord Illingworth. Dear Dr. Daubeny, our rector here, provides, with the assistance of his curates, really admirable recreations for the poor during the winter. And much good may be done by means of a magic lantern, or a missionary, or some popular amusement of that kind.

Lady Caroline: I am not at all in favour of amusements for the poor, Jane. Blankets and coals are sufficient. There is too much love of pleasure amongst the upper classes as it is. Health is what we want in modern life. The tone is not healthy, not healthy at all.

Kelvil: You are quite right, Lady Caroline.

Lady Caroline: I believe I am usually right.

Mrs. Allonby: Horrid word 'health.'

Lord Illingworth: Silliest word in our language, and one knows so well the popular idea of health. The English country gentleman galloping after a fox – the unspeakable in full pursuit of the uneatable.

Kelvil: May I ask, Lord Illingworth, if you regard the House of Lords as a better institution than the House of Commons?

Lord Illingworth: A much better institution, of course. We in the House of Lords are never in touch with public opinion. That makes us a civilised body.

Kelvil: Are you serious in putting forward such a view?

Lord Illingworth: Quite serious, Mr. Kelvil. (*To* MRS. ALLONBY.) Vulgar habit that is people have nowadays of asking one, after one has given them an idea, whether one is serious or not. Nothing is serious except passion. The intellect is not a serious thing, and never has been. It is an instrument on which one plays, that is all. The only serious form of intellect I know is the British intellect. And on the British intellect the illiterates play the drum.

Lady Hunstanton: What are you saying, Lord Illingworth, about the drum?

Lord Illingworth: I was merely talking to Mrs. Allonby about the leading articles in the London newspapers.

Lady Hunstanton: But do you believe all that is written in the newspapers?

Lord Illingworth: I do. Nowadays it is only the unreadable that occurs. (*Rises with* MRS. ALLONBY.)

Lady Hunstanton: Are you going, Mrs. Allonby?

Mrs. Allonby: Just as far as the conservatory. Lord Illingworth told me this morning that there was an orchid there as beautiful as the seven deadly sins.

Lady Hunstanton: My dear, I hope there is nothing of the kind. I will certainly speak to the gardener.

Exit MRS. ALLONBY *and* LORD ILLINGWORTH.

Lady Caroline: Remarkable type, Mrs. Allonby.

Lady Hunstanton: She lets her clever tongue run away with her sometimes.

Lady Caroline: Is that the only thing, Jane, Mrs. Allonby allows to run away with her?

Lady Hunstanton: I hope so, Caroline, I am sure.

Enter LORD ALFRED.

Dear Lord Alfred, do join us.

LORD ALFRED *sits down beside* LADY STUTFIELD.

Lady Caroline: You believe good of every one, Jane. It is a great fault.

Lady Stutfield: Do you really, really think, Lady Caroline, that one should believe evil of every one?

Lady Caroline: I think it is much safer to do so, Lady Stutfield. Until, of course, people are found out to be good. But that requires a great deal of investigation nowadays.

Lady Stutfield: But there is so much unkind scandal in modern life.

Lady Caroline: Lord Illingworth remarked to me last night at dinner that the basis of every scandal is an absolutely immoral certainty.

Kelvil: Lord Illingworth is, of course, a very brilliant man, but he seems to me to be lacking in that fine faith in the nobility and purity of life which is so important in this century.

Lady Stutfield: Yes, quite, quite important, is it not?

Kelvil: He gives me the impression of a man who does not appreciate the beauty of our English home-life. I would say that he was tainted with foreign ideas on the subject.

Lady Stutfield: There is nothing, nothing like the beauty of home-life, is there?

Kelvil: It is the mainstay of our moral system in England, Lady Stutfield. Without it we would become like our neighbours.

Lady Stutfield: That would be so, so sad, would it not?

Kelvil: I am afraid, too, that Lord Illingworth regards woman simply as a toy. Now, I have never regarded woman as a toy. Woman is the intellectual helpmeet of man in public as in private life. Without her we should forget the true ideals. (*Sits down beside* LADY STUTFIELD.)

Lady Stutfield: I am so very, very glad to hear you say that.

Lady Caroline: You a married man, Mr. Kettle?

Sir John: Kelvil, dear, Kelvil.

Kelvil: I am married, Lady Caroline.

Lady Caroline: Family?

Kelvil: Yes.

Lady Caroline: How many?

Kelvil: Eight.

LADY STUTFIELD *turns her attention to* LORD ALFRED.

Lady Caroline: Mrs. Kettle and the children are, I suppose, at the seaside?

SIR JOHN *shrugs his shoulders.*

Kelvil: My wife is at the seaside with the children, Lady Caroline.

Lady Caroline: You will join them later on, no doubt?

Kelvil: If my public engagements permit me.

Lady Caroline: Your public life must be a great source of gratification to Mrs. Kettle.

Sir John: Kelvil, my love, Kelvil.

Lady Stutfield (*to* LORD ALFRED): How very, very charming those gold-tipped cigarettes of yours are, Lord Alfred.

Lord Alfred: They are awfully expensive. I can only afford them when I'm in debt.

Lady Stutfield: It must be terribly, terribly distressing to be in debt.

Lord Alfred: One must have some occupation nowadays. If I hadn't my debts I shouldn't have anything to think about. All the chaps I know are in debt.

Lady Stutfield: But don't the people to whom you owe the money give you a great, great deal of annoyance?

Enter Footman.

Lord Alfred: Oh, no, they write. I don't.

Lady Stutfield: How very, very strange.

Lady Hunstanton: Ah, here is a letter, Caroline, from dear Mrs. Arbuthnot. She won't dine. I am so sorry. But she will come in the evening. I am very pleased, indeed. She is one of the sweetest of women. Writes a beautiful hand, too, so large, so firm. (*Hands letter to* LADY CAROLINE.)

Lady Caroline (looking at it): A little lacking in femininity, Jane. Femininity is the quality I admire most in women.

Lady Hunstanton (taking back letter and leaving it on table): Oh ! she is very feminine, Caroline, and so good, too. You should hear what the Archdeacon says of her. He regards her as his right hand in the parish. (*Footman speaks to her.*) In the Yellow Drawing-room. Shall we all go in? Lady Stutfield, shall we go in to tea?

Lady Stutfield: With pleasure, Lady Hunstanton.

They rise and proceed to go off. SIR JOHN *offers to carry* LADY STUTFIELD'S *cloak.*

Lady Caroline: John! If you would allow your nephew to look after Lady Stutfield's cloak, you might help me with my work-basket.

Enter LORD ILLINGWORTH and MRS. ALLONBY.

Sir John: Certainly, my love.

Exeut.

Mrs. Allonby: Curious thing, plain women are always jealous of their husbands, beautiful women never are!

Lord Illingworth: Beautiful women never have time. They are always so occupied in being jealous of other people's husbands.

Mrs. Allonby: I should have thought Lady Caroline would have grown tired of conjugal anxiety by this time! Sir John is her fourth !

Lord Illingworth: So much marriage is certainly not becoming. Twenty years of romance make a woman look like a ruin; but twenty years of marriage make her something like a public building.

Mrs. Allonby: Twenty years of romance! Is there such a thing?

Lord Illingworth: Not in our day. Women have become too brilliant. Nothing spoils a romance so much as a sense of humour in the woman.

Mrs. Allonby: Or the want of it in the man.

Lord Illingworth: You are quite right. In a Temple every one should be serious, except the thing that is worshipped.

Mrs. Allonby: And that should be man?

Lord Illingworth: Women kneel so gracefully; men don't.

Mrs. Allonby: You are thinking of Lady Stutfield !

Lord Illingworth: I assure you I have not thought of Lady Stutfield for the last quarter of an hour.

Mrs. Allonby: Is she such a mystery?

Lord Illingworth: She is more than a mystery – she is a mood.

Mrs. Allonby: Moods don't last.

Lord Illingworth: It is their chief charm.

Enter HESTER *and* GERALD.

Gerald: Lord Illingworth, every one has been congratulating me, Lady Hunstanton and Lady Caroline, and. . . every one. I hope I shall make a good secretary.

Lord Illingworth: You will be the pattern secretary Gerald. (*Talks to him.*)

Mrs. Allonby: You enjoy country life, Miss Worsley?

Hester: Very much indeed.

Mrs. Allonby: Don't find yourself longing for a London dinner-party?

Hester: I dislike London dinner-parties.

Mrs. Allonby: I adore them. The clever people never listen, and the stupid people never talk.

Hester: I think the stupid people talk a great deal.

Mrs. Allonby: Ah, I never listen!

Lord Illingworth: My dear boy, if I didn't like you I wouldn't have made you the offer. It is because I like you so much that I want to have you with me.

Exit HESTER *with* GERALD.

Charming fellow, Gerald Arbuthnot!
Mrs. Allonby: He is very nice; very nice indeed. But I can't stand the American young lady.
Lord Illingworth: Why?
Mrs. Allonby: She told me yesterday, and in quite a loud voice too, that she was only eighteen. It was most annoying.
Lord Illingworth: One should never trust a woman who tells one her real age. A woman who would tell one that, would tell one anything.
Mrs. Allonby: She is a Puritan besides –
Lord Illingworth: Ah, that is inexcusable. I don't mind plain women being Puritans. It is the only excuse they have for being plain. But she is decidedly pretty. I admire her immensely. (*Looks steadfastly at* MRS. ALLONBY.)
Mrs. Allonby: What a thoroughly bad man you must be!
Lord Illingworth: What do you call a bad man?
Mrs. Allonby: The sort of man who admires innocence.
Lord Illingworth: And a bad woman?
Mrs. Allonby: Oh ! the sort of woman a man never gets tired of.
Lord Illingworth: You are severe – on yourself.
Mrs. Allonby: Define us as a sex.
Lord Illingworth: Sphinxes without secrets.
Mrs. Allonby: Does that include the Puritan women?
Lord Illingworth: Do you know, I don't believe in the existence of Puritan women? I don't think there is a woman in the world who would not be a little flattered if one made love to her. It is that which makes women so irresistibly adorable.
Mrs. Allonby: You think there is no woman in the world who would object to being kissed?
Lord Illingworth: Very few.
Mrs. Allonby: Miss Worsley would not let you kiss her.
Lord Illingworth: Are you sure?
Mrs. Allonby: Quite.
Lord Illingworth: What do you think she'd do if I kissed her?
Mrs. Allonby: Either marry you, or strike you across the face with her glove. What would you do if she struck you across the face with her glove?
Lord Illingworth: Fall in love with her, probably.
Mrs. Allonby: Then it is lucky you are not going to kiss her!
Lord Illingworth: Is that a challenge?

Mrs. Allonby: It is an arrow shot into the air.

Lord Illingworth: Don't you know that I always succeed in whatever I try?

Mrs. Allonby: I am sorry to hear it. We women adore failures. They lean on us.

Lord Illingworth: You worship successes. You cling to them.

Mrs. Allonby: We are the laurels to hide their baldness.

Lord Illingworth: And they need you always, except at the moment of triumph.

Mrs. Allonby: They are uninteresting then.

Lord Illingworth: How tantalising you are? (*A pause.*)

Mrs. Allonby: Lord Illingworth, there is one thing I shall always like you for.

Lord Illingworth: Only one thing? And I have so many bad qualities.

Mrs. Allonby: Ah, don't be too conceited about them. You may lose them as you grow old.

Lord Illingworth: I never intend to grow old. The soul is born old but grows young. That is the comedy of life.

Mrs. Allonby: And the body is born young and grows old. That is life's tragedy.

Lord Illingworth: Its comedy also, sometimes. But what is the mysterious reason why you will always like me?

Mrs. Allonby: It is that you have never made love to me.

Lord Illingworth: I have never done anything else.

Mrs. Allonby: Really? I have not noticed it.

Lord Illingworth: How unfortunate! It might have been a tragedy for both of us.

Mrs. Allonby: We should each have survived.

Lord Illingworth: One can survive everything nowadays, except death, and live down anything except a good reputation.

Mrs. Allonby: Have you tried a good reputation?

Lord Illingworth: It is one of the many annoyances to which I have never been subjected.

Mrs. Allonby: It may come.

Lord Illingworth: Why do you threaten me?

Mrs. Allonby: I will tell you when you have kissed the Puritan.

Enter Footman.

Francis: Tea is served in the Yellow-Drawing-room, my lord.

Lord Illingworth: Tell her ladyship we are coming in.

Francis: Yes, my lord. (*Exit.*)

Lord Illingworth: Shall we go in to tea?

Mrs. Allonby: Do you like such simple pleasures?

Lord Illingworth: I adore simple pleasures. They are the last refuge of the complex. But, if you wish, let us stay here. Yes, let us stay here. The Book of Life begins with a man and a woman in a garden.

Mrs. Allonby: It ends with Revelations.

Lord Illingworth: You fence divinely. But the button has come off your foil.

Mrs. Allonby: I have still the mask.

Lord Illingworth: It makes your eyes lovelier.

Mrs. Allonby: Thank you. Come.

Lord Illingworth (*sees* MRS. ARBUTHNOT'S *letter on table, and takes it up and looks at envelope*): What a curious handwriting! It reminds me of the handwriting of a woman I used to know years ago.

Mrs. Allonby: Who?

Lord Illingworth: Oh! no one. No one in particular. A woman of no importance. (*Throws letter down, and passes up the steps of the terrace with* MRS. ALLONBY. *They smile at each other.*)

ACT DROP.

SECOND ACT

SCENE

Drawing-room at Hunstanton, after dinner lamps lit. Door L.C. Door R.C.

Ladies seated on sofa.

Mrs. Allonby: What a comfort it is to have got rid of the men for a little!

Lady Stutfield: Yes; men persecute us dreadfully, don't they?

Mrs. Allonby: Persecute us? I wish they did.

Lady Hunstanton: My dear!

Mrs. Allonby: The annoying thing is that the wretches can be perfectly happy without us. That is why I think it is every woman's duty never to leave them alone for a single moment, except during this short breathing space after dinner; without which, I believe, we poor women would be absolutely worn to shadows.

Enter Servants with coffee.

Lady Hunstanton: Worn to shadows, dear?

Mrs. Allonby: Yes, Lady Hunstanton. It is such a strain keeping men up to the mark. They are always trying to escape from us.

Lady Stutfield: It seems to me that it is we who are always trying to escape from them. Men are so very, very heartless. They know their power and use it.

Lady Caroline (takes coffee from Servant): What stuff and nonsense all this about men is! The thing to do is to keep men in their proper place.

Mrs. Allonby: But what is their proper place, Lady Caroline?

Lady Caroline: Looking after their wives, Mrs. Allonby.

Mrs. Allonby (takes coffee from Servant): Really. And if they're not married?

Lady Caroline: If they are not married, they should be looking after a wife. It's perfectly scandalous, the amount of bachelors who are going about society. There should be a law passed to compel them all to marry within twelve months.

Lady Stutfield (refuses coffee): But if they're in love with some one who, perhaps, is tied to another?

Lady Caroline: In that case, Lady Stutfield, they would be married off in a week to some plain respectable girl, in order to teach them not to meddle with other people's property.

Mrs. Allonby: I don't think that we should ever be spoken of as other people's property. All men are married women's property. That is the only true definition of what married women's property really is. But we don't belong to any one.

Lady Stutfield: Oh, I am so very, very glad to hear you say so.

Lady Hunstanton: But do you really think, dear Caroline, that legislation would improve matters in any way? I am told that, nowadays, all the married men live like bachelors, and all the bachelors like married men.

Mrs. Allonby: I certainly never know one from the other.

Lady Stutfield: Oh, I think one can always know at once whether a man has home claims upon his life or not. I have noticed a very, very sad expression in the eyes of so many married men.

Mrs. Allonby: Ah, all that I have noticed is that they are horribly tedious when they are good husbands, and abominably conceited when they are not.

Lady Hunstanton: Well, I suppose the type of husband has completely changed since my young days, but I am bound to state that poor dear Hunstanton was the most delightful of creatures, and as good as gold.

Mrs. Allonby: Ah, my husband is a sort of promise note; I'm tired of meeting him.

Lady Caroline: But you renew him from time to time, don't you?

Mrs. Allonby: Oh no, Lady Caroline. I have only had one husband as yet. I suppose you look upon me as quite an amateur.

Lady Caroline: With your views on life I wonder you married at all.

Mrs. Allonby: So do I.

Lady Hunstanton: My dear child, I believe you are really very happy in your married life, but that you like to hide your happiness from others.

Mrs. Allonby: I assure you I was horribly deceived in Ernest.

Lady Hunstanton: Oh, I hope not, dear. I knew his mother quite well. She was a Stratton, Caroline, one of Lord Crowland's daughters.

Lady Caroline: Victoria Stratton? I remember her perfectly. A silly, fair-haired woman with no chin.

Mrs. Allonby: Ah, Ernest has a chin. He has a very strong chin, a square chin. Ernest's chin is far too square.

Lady Stutfield: But do you really think a man's chin can be too square? I think a man should look very, very strong, and that his chin should be quite, quite square.

Mrs. Allonby: Then you should certainly know Ernest, Lady Stutfield. It is only fair to tell you beforehand he has got no conversation at all.

Lady Stutfield: I adore silent men.

Mrs. Allonby: Oh, Ernest isn't silent. He talks the whole time. But he has got no conversation. What he talks about I don't know. I haven't listened to him for years.

Lady Stutfield: Have you never forgiven him then? How sad that seems! But all life is very, very sad, is it not?

Mrs. Allonby: Life, Lady Stutfield, is simply a *mauvais quart d'heure* made up of exquisite moments.

Lady Stutfield: Yes, there are moments, certainly. But was it something very, very wrong that Mr. Allonby did? Did he become angry with you, and say anything that was unkind or true?

Mrs. Allonby: Oh, dear, no. Ernest is invariably calm. That is one of the reasons he always gets on my nerves. Nothing is so aggravating as calmness. There is something positively brutal about the good temper of most modern men. I wonder we women stand it as well as we do.

Lady Stutfield: Yes; men's good temper shows they are not so sensitive as we are, not so finely strung. It makes a great barrier often between husband and wife, does it not? But I would so much like to know what was the wrong thing Mr. Allonby did.

Mrs. Allonby: Well, I will tell you, if you solemnly promise to tell everybody else.

Lady Stutfield: Thank you, thank you. I will make a point of repeating it.

Mrs. Allonby: When Ernest and I were engaged, he swore to me positively on his knees that he had never loved any one before in the whole course of his life. I was very young at the time, so I didn't believe him, I needn't tell you. Unfortunately, however, I made no inquiries of any kind till after I had been actually married four or five months. I found out then that what he had told me was perfectly true. And that sort of thing makes a man so absolutely uninteresting.

Lady Hunstanton: My dear!

Mrs. Allonby: Men always want to be a woman's first love. That is their clumsy vanity. We women have a more subtle instinct about things. What we like is to be a man's last romance.

Lady Stutfield: I see what you mean. It's very, very beautiful.

Lady Hunstanton: My dear child, you don't mean to tell me that you won't forgive your husband because he never loved any one else? Did you ever hear such a thing, Caroline? I am quite surprised.

Lady Caroline: Oh, women have become so highly educated, Jane, that nothing should surprise us nowadays, except happy marriages. They apparently are getting remarkably rare.

Mrs. Allonby: Oh, they're quite out of date.

Lady Stutfield: Except amongst the middle classes, I have been told.

Mrs. Allonby: How like the middle classes!

Lady Stutfield: Yes – is it not? – very, very like them.

Lady Caroline: If what you tell us about the middle classes is true, Lady Stutfield, it redounds greatly to their credit. It is much to be regretted that in our rank of life the wife should be so persistently frivolous, under the impression apparently that it is the proper thing to be. It is to that I attribute the unhappiness of so many marriages we all know of in society.

Mrs. Allonby: Do you know, Lady Caroline, I don't think the frivolity of the wife has ever anything to do with it. More marriages are ruined nowadays by the common sense of the husband than by anything else. How can a woman be expected to be happy with a man who insists on treating her as if she was a perfectly rational being?

Lady Hunstanton: My dear!

Mrs. Allonby: Man, poor, awkward, reliable, necessary man belongs to a sex that has been rational for millions and millions of years. He can't help himself. It is in his race. The History of Woman is very different. We have always been picturesque protests against the mere existence of common sense. We saw its dangers from the first.

Lady Stutfield: Yes, the common sense of husbands is certainly most, most trying. Do tell me your conception of the Ideal Husband. I think it would be so very, very helpful.

Mrs. Allonby: The Ideal Husband? There couldn't be such a thing. The institution is wrong.

Lady Stutfield: The Ideal Man, then, in his relations to *us*.

Lady Caroline: He would probably be extremely realistic.

Mrs. Allonby: The Ideal Man! Oh, the Ideal Man should talk to us as if we were goddesses, and treat us as if we were children. He should refuse all our serious requests, and gratify every one of our whims. He should encourage us to have caprices, and forbid us to have missions. He should always say much more than he means, and always mean much more than he says.

Lady Hunstanton: But how could he do both, dear?

Mrs. Allonby: He should never run down other pretty women. That would show he had no taste, or make one suspect that he had too much. No, he should be nice about them all, but say that somehow they don't attract him.

Lady Stutfield: Yes, that is always very, very pleasant to hear about other women.

Mrs. Allonby: If we ask him a question about anything, he should give us an answer all about ourselves. He should invariably praise us for whatever qualities he knows we haven't got. But he should be pitiless, quite pitiless, in reproaching us for the virtues that we have never dreamed of possessing. He should never believe that we know the use of useful things. That would be unforgivable. But he should shower on us everything we don't want.

Lady Caroline: As far as I can see, he is to do nothing but pay bills and compliments.

Mrs. Allonby: He should persistently compromise us in public, and treat us with absolute respect when we are alone. And yet he should be always ready to have a perfectly terrible scene, whenever we want one, and to become miserable, absolutely miserable, at a moment's notice, and to overwhelm us with just reproaches in less than twenty minutes, and to be positively violent at the end of half an hour, and to leave us for ever at a quarter to eight, when we have to go and dress for dinner. And when, after that, one has seen him for really the last time, and he has refused to take back the little things he has given one, and promised never to communicate with one again, or to write one any foolish letters, he should be perfectly broken-hearted, and telegraph to one all day long, and send one little notes every half-hour by a private hansom, and dine quite alone at the club, so that every one should know how unhappy he was. And after a whole dreadful week, during which one has gone about everywhere with one's husband, just to show how absolutely lonely one was, he may be given a third last parting, in the evening, and then, if his conduct has been quite irreproachable, and one has behaved really badly to him, he should be allowed to admit that he has been entirely in the wrong, and when he has admitted that, it becomes a woman's duty to forgive, and one can do it all over again from the beginning, with variations.

Lady Hunstanton: How clever you are, my dear! You never mean a single word you say.

Lady Stutfield: Thank you, thank you. It has been quite, quite entrancing. I must try and remember it all. There are such a number of details that are so very, very important.

Lady Caroline: But you have not told us yet what the reward of the Ideal Man is to be.

Mrs. Allonby: His reward? Oh, infinite expectation. That is quite enough for him.

Lady Stutfield: But men are so terribly, terribly exacting, are they not?

Mrs. Allonby: That makes no matter. One should never surrender.

Lady Stutfield: Not even to the Ideal Man?

Mrs. Allonby: Certainly not to him. Unless, of course, one wants to grow tired of him.

Lady Stutfield: Oh! . . . Yes. I see that. It is very, very helpful. Do you think, Mrs. Allonby, I shall every meet the Ideal Man? Or are there more than one?

Mrs. Allonby: There are just four in London, Lady Stutfield.

Lady Hunstanton: Oh, my dear!

Mrs. Allonby (going over to her): What has happened? Do tell me.

Lady Hunstanton (in a low voice): I had completely forgotten that the American young lady has been in the room all the time. I am afraid some of this clever talk may have shocked her a little.

Mrs. Allonby: Ah, that will do her so much good!

Lady Hunstanton: Let us hope she didn't understand much. I think I had better go over and talk to her. (*Rises and goes across to* HESTER WORSLEY.) Well, dear Miss Worsley. (*Sitting down beside her.*) How quiet you have been in your nice little corner all this time! I suppose you have been reading a book? There are so many books here in the library.

Hester: No, I have been listening to the conversation.

Lady Hunstanton: You mustn't believe everything that was said, you know, dear.

Hester: I didn't believe any of it.

Lady Hunstanton: That is quite right, dear.

Hester (continuing): I couldn't believe that any women could really hold such views of life as I have heard to-night from some of your guests. (*An awkward pause.*)

Lady Hunstanton: I hear you have such pleasant society in America. Quite like our own in places, my son wrote to me.

Hester: There are cliques in America as elsewhere, Lady Hunstanton. But true American society consists simply of all the good women and good men we have in our country.

Lady Hunstanton: What a sensible system, and I dare say quite pleasant, too. I am afraid in England we have too many artificial social barriers. We don't see as much as we should of the middle and lower classes.

Hester: In America we have no lower classes.

Lady Hunstanton: Really? What a very strange arrangement!

Mrs. Allonby: What is that dreadful girl talking about?

Lady Stutfield: She is painfully natural, is she not?

Lady Caroline: There are a great many things you haven't got in America, I am told, Miss Worsley. They say you have no ruins, and no curiosities.

Mrs. Allonby (to LADY STUTFIELD): What nonsense! They have their mothers and their manners.

Hester: The English aristocracy supply us with our curiosities, Lady Caroline. They are sent over to us every summer, regularly, in the steamers, and propose to us the day after they land. As for ruins, we are trying to build up something that will last longer than brick or stone. (*Gets up to take her fan from table.*)

Lady Hunstanton: What is that, dear? Ah, yes, an iron Exhibition, is it not, at that place that has the curious name?

Hester (*standing by table*): We are trying to build up life, Lady Hunstanton, on a better, truer, purer basis than life rests on here. This sounds strange to you all, no doubt. How could it sound other than strange? You rich people in England, you don't know how you are living. How could you know? You shut out from your society the gentle and the good. You laugh at the simple and the pure. Living, as you all do, on others and by them, you sneer at self-sacrifice, and if you throw bread to the poor, it is merely to keep them quiet for a season. With all your pomp and wealth and art you don't know how to live – you don't even know that. You love the beauty that you can see and touch and handle, the beauty that you can destroy, and do destroy, but of the unseen beauty of life, of the unseen beauty of a higher life, you know nothing. You have lost life's secret. Oh, your English society seems to me shallow, selfish, foolish. It has blinded its eyes, and stopped its ears. It lies like a leper in purple. It sits like a dead thing smeared with gold. It is all wrong, all wrong.

Lady Stutfield: I don't think one should know of these things. It is not very, very nice, is it?

Lady Hunstanton: My dear Miss Worsley, I thought you liked

English society so much. You were such a success in it. And you were so much admired by the best people. I quite forget what Lord Henry Weston said of you – but it was most complimentary, and you know what an authority he is on beauty.

Hester: Lord Henry Weston! I remember him, Lady Hunstanton. A man with a hideous smile and a hideous past. He is asked everywhere. No dinner party is complete without him. What of those whose ruin is due to him? They are outcasts. They are nameless. If you met them in the street you would turn your head away. I don't complain of their punishment. Let all women who have sinned be punished.

MRS. ARBUTHNOT *enters from terrace behind in a cloak with a lace veil over her head. She hears the last words and starts.*

Lady Hunstanton: My dear young lady!
Hester: It is right that they should be punished, but don't let them be the only ones to suffer. If a man and woman have sinned, let them both go forth into the desert to love or loathe each other there. Let them both be branded. Set a mark, if you wish, on each, but don't punish the one and let the other go free. Don't have one law for men and another for women. You are unjust to women in England. And till you count what is a shame in a woman to be infamy in a man, you will always be unjust, and Right, that pillar of fire, and Wrong, that pillar of cloud, will be made dim to your eyes, or be not seen at all, or if seen, not regarded.

Lady Caroline: Might I, dear Miss Worsley, as you are standing up, ask you for my cotton that is just behind you? Thank you.
Lady Hunstanton: My dear Mrs. Arbuthnot! I am so pleased you have come up. But I didn't hear you announced.
Mrs. Arbuthnot: Oh, I came straight in from the terrace, Lady Hunstanton, just as I was. You didn't tell me you had a party.
Lady Hunstanton: Not a party. Only a few guests who are staying in the house, and whom you must know. Allow me. (*Tries to help her. Rings bell.*) Caroline, this is Mrs. Arbuthnot, one of my sweetest friends. Lady Caroline Pontefract, Lady Stutfield, Mrs. Allonby, amd my young American friend, Miss Worsley, who has just been telling us all how wicked we are.
Hester: I am afraid you think I spoke too strongly, Lady Hunstanton. But there are some things in England –
Lady Hunstanton: My dear young lady, there was a great deal of truth, I dare say, in what you said, and you looked very pretty while you said it, which is much more important, Lord Illingworth would

tell us. The only point where I thought you were a little hard was about Lady Caroline's brother, about poor Lord Henry. He is really such good company.

Enter Footman.

Take Mrs. Arbuthnot's things.

Exit Footman with wraps.

Hester: Lady Caroline, I had no idea it was your brother. I am sorry for the pain I must have caused you – I –

Lady Caroline: My dear Miss Worsley, the only part of your little speech, if I may so term it, with which I thoroughly agreed, was the part about my brother. Nothing that you could possibly say could be too bad for him. I regard Henry as infamous, absolutely infamous. But I am bound to state, as you were remarking, Jane, that he is excellent company, and he has one of the best cooks in London, and after a good dinner one can forgive anybody, even one's own relations.

Lady Hunstanton (*to* MISS WORSLEY): Now, do come, dear, and make friends with Mrs. Arbuthnot. She is one of the good, sweet, simple people you told us we never admitted into society. I am sorry to say Mrs. Arbuthnot comes very rarely to me. But that is not my fault.

Mrs. Allonby: What a bore it is the men staying so long after dinner! I expect they are saying the most dreadful things about us.

Lady Stutfield: Do you really think so?

Mrs. Allonby: I am sure of it.

Lady Stutfield: How very, very horrid of them! Shall we go on to the terrace?

Mrs. Allonby: Oh, anything to get away from the dowagers and the dowdies. (*Rises and goes with* LADY STUTFIELD *to door L.C.*) We are only going to look at the stars, Lady Hunstanton.

Lady Hunstanton: You will find a great many, dear, a great many. But don't catch cold. (*To* MRS. ARBUTHNOT): We shall all miss Gerald so much, dear Mrs Arbuthnot.

Mrs. Arbuthnot: But has Lord Illingworth really offered to make Gerald his secretary?

Lady Hunstanton: Oh, yes! He has been most charming about it. He has the highest possible opinion of your boy. You don't know Lord Illingworth, I believe, dear.

Mrs. Arbuthnot: I have never met him.

Lady Hunstanton: You know him by name, no doubt?

Mrs. Arbuthnot: I am afraid I don't. I live so much out of the world, and see so few people. I remember hearing years ago of an old Lord Illingworth who lived in Yorkshire, I think.

Lady Hunstanton: Ah, yes. That would be the last Earl but one. He was a very curious man. He wanted to marry beneath him. Or wouldn't, I believe. There was some scandal about it. The present Lord Illingworth is quite different. He is very distinguished. He does – well, he does nothing, which I am afraid our pretty American visitor here thinks very wrong of anybody, and I don't know that he cares much for the subjects in which you are so interested, dear Mrs. Arbuthnot. Do you think, Caroline, that Lord Illingworth is interested in the Housing of the Poor?

Lady Caroline: I should fancy not at all, Jane.

Lady Hunstanton: We all have our different tastes have we not? But Lord Illingworth has a very high position, and there is nothing he couldn't get if he chose to ask for it. Of course, he is comparatively a young man still, and he has only come to his title within – how long exactly is it, Caroline, since Lord Illingworth succeeded?

Lady Caroline: About four years, I think, Jane. I know it was the same year in which my brother had his last exposure in the evening newspapers.

Lady Hunstanton: Ah, I remember. That would be about four years ago. Of course, there were a great many people between the present Lord Illingworth and the title, Mrs. Arbuthnot. There was – who was there, Caroline?

Lady Caroline: There was poor Margaret's baby. You remember how anxious she was, to have a boy, and it was a boy, but it died, and her husband died shortly afterwards, and she married almost immediately one of Lord Ascot's sons, who, I am told, beats her.

Lady Hunstanton: Ah, that is in the family, dear, that is in the family. And there was also, I remember, a clergyman who wanted to be a lunatic, or a lunatic who wanted to be a clergyman, I forget which, but I know the Court of Chancery investigated the matter, and decided that he was quite sane. And I saw him afterwards at poor Lord Plumstead's with straws in his hair, or something very odd about him. I can't recall what. I often regret, Lady Caroline, that dear Lady Cecilia never lived to see her son get the title.

Mrs. Arbuthnot: Lady Cecilia?

Lady Hunstanton: Lord Illingworth's mother, dear Mrs. Arbuthnot, was one of the Duchess of Jerningham's pretty daughters, and she married Sir Thomas Harford, who wasn't considered a very good match for her at the time, though he was said to be the handsomest man in London. I knew them all quite intimately, and both the sons, Arthur and George.

Mrs. Arbuthnot: It was the eldest son who succeeded, of course, Lady Hunstanton?

Lady Hunstanton: No, dear, he was killed in the hunting field. Or was it fishing, Caroline? I forget. But George came in for everything. I always tell him that no younger son has ever had such good luck as he has had.

Mrs. Arbuthnot: Lady Hunstanton, I want to speak to Gerald at once. Might I see him? Can he be sent for?

Lady Hunstanton: Certainly, dear. I will send one of the servants into the dining-room to fetch him. I don't know what keeps the gentlemen so long. (*Rings bell.*) When I knew Lord Illingworth first as plain George Harford, he was simply a very brilliant young man about town, with not a penny of money except what poor dear Lady Cecilia gave him. She was quite devoted to him. Chiefly, I fancy, because he was on bad terms with his father. Oh, here is the dear Archdeacon. (*To Servan.*) It doesn't matter.

Enter SIR JOHN *and* DOCTOR DAUBENY. SIR JOHN *goes over to* LADY STUTFIELD, DOCTOR DAUBENY *to* LADY HUNSTANTON.

The Archdeacon: Lord Illingworth has been most entertaining. I have never enjoyed myself more. (*Sees* MRS. ARBUTHNOT.) Ah, Mrs. Arbuthnot.

Lady Hunstanton (*to* DOCTOR DAUBENY): You see I have got Mrs. Arbuthnot to come to me at last.

The Archdeacon: That is a great honour, Lady Hunstanton. Mrs. Daubeny will be quite jealous of you.

Lady Hunstanton: Ah, I am so sorry Mrs. Daubeny could not come with you to-night. Headache as usual, I suppose.

The Archdeacon: Yes, Lady Hunstanton; a perfect martyr. But she is happiest alone. She is happiest alone.

Lady Caroline (*to her husband*): John!

SIR JOHN *goes over to his wife.* DOCTOR DAUBENY *talks to* LADY HUNSTANTON *and* MRS. ARBUTHNOT.

MRS. ARBUTHNOT *watches* LORD ILLINGWORTH *the whole time. He has passed across the room without noticing her, and approaches* MRS. ALLONBY, *who with* LADY STUTFIELD *is standing by the door looking on to the terrace.*

Lord Illingworth: How is the most charming woman in the world?

Mrs. Allonby (taking LADY STUTFIELD *by the hand):* We are both quite well, thank you, Lord Illingworth. But what a short time you have been in the dining-room! It seems as if we had only just left.

Lord Illingworth: I was bored to death. Never opened my lips the whole time. Absolutely longing to come in to you.

Mrs. Allonby: You should have. The American girl has been giving us a lecture.

Lord Illingworth: Really? All Americans lecture, I believe. I suppose it is something in their climate. What did she lecture about?

Mrs. Allonby: Oh, Puritanism, of course.

Lord Illingworth: I am going to convert her, am I not? How long do you give me?

Mrs. Allonby: A week.

Lord Illingworth: A week is more than enough.

Enter GERALD *and* LORD ALFRED.

Gerald (going to MRS. ARBUTHNOT): Dear mother!

Mrs. Arbuthnot: Gerald, I don't feel at all well. See me home, Gerald. I shouldn't have come.

Gerald: I am so sorry, mother. Certainly. But you must know Lord Illingworth first. *(Goes across room.)*

Mrs. Arbuthnot: Not to-night, Gerald.

Gerald: Lord Illingworth, I want you so much to know my mother.

Lord Illingworth: With the greatest pleasure. *(To* MRS. ALLONBY.) I'll be back in a moment. People's mothers always bore me to death. All women become like their mothers. That is their tragedy.

Mrs. Allonby: No man does. That is his.

Lord Illingworth: What a delightful mood you are in to-night! *(Turns round and goes across with* GERALD *to* MRS. ARBUTHNOT. *When he sees her, he starts back in wonder. Then slowly his eyes turn towards* GERALD.)

Gerald: Mother, this is Lord Illingworth, who has offered to take me as his private secretary.

MRS. ARBUTHNOT *bows coldly.*

It is a wonderful opening for me, isn't it? I hope he won't be disappointed in me, that is all. You'll thank Lord Illingworth, mother, won't you?

Mrs. Arbuthnot: Lord Illingworth is very good, I am sure, to interest himself in you for the moment.

Lord Illingworth (putting his hand on GERALD'S *shoulder):* Oh, Gerald and I are great friends already, Mrs. . . . Arbuthnot.

Mrs. Arbuthnot: There can be nothing in common between you and my son, Lord Illingworth.

Gerald: Dear mother, how can you say so? Of course, Lord Illingworth is awfully clever and that sort of thing. There is nothing Lord Illingworth doesn't know.

Lord Illingworth: My dear boy!

Gerald: He knows more about life than any one I have ever met. I feel an awful duffer when I am with you, Lord Illingworth. Of course, I have had so few advantages. I have not been to Eton or Oxford like other chaps. But Lord Illingworth doesn't seem to mind that. He had been awfully good to me, mother.

Mrs. Arbuthnot: Lord Illingworth may change his mind. He may not really want you as his secretary.

Gerald: Mother!

Mrs. Arbuthnot: You must remember, as you said yourself, you have had so few advantages.

Mrs. Allonby: Lord Illingworth, I want to speak to you for a moment. Do come over.

Lord Illingworth: Will you excuse me, Mrs. Arbuthnot? Now, don't let your charming mother make any more difficulties, Gerald. The thing is quite settled, isn't it?

Gerald: I hope so.

LORD ILLINGWORTH goes across to MRS. ALLONBY.

Mrs. Allonby: I thought you were never going to leave the lady in black velvet.

Lord Illingworth: She is excessively handsome. (*Looks at* MRS. ARBUTHNOT.)

Lady Hunstanton: Caroline, shall we all make a move to the music-room? Miss Worsley is going to play. You'll come too, dear Mrs. Arbuthnot, won't you? You don't know what a treat is in store for you. (*To* DOCTOR DAUBENY.) I must really take Miss

Worsley down some afternoon to the rectory. I should so much like dear Mrs. Daubeny to hear her on the violin. Ah, I forgot. Dear Mrs. Daubeny's hearing is a little defective, is it not?

The Archdeacon: Her deafness is a great privation to her. She can't even hear my sermons now. She reads them at home. But she has many resources in herself, many resources.

Lady Hunstanton: She reads a good deal, I suppose?

The Archdeacon: Just the very largest print. The eyesight is rapidly going. But she's never morbid, never morbid.

Gerald (to Lord Illingworth.) Do speak to my mother, Lord Illingworth, before you go into the music-room. She seems to think, somehow, you don't mean what you said to me.

Mrs. Allonby: Aren't you coming?

Lord Illingworth: In a few moments. Lady Hunstanton, if Mrs. Arbuthnot would allow me, I would like to say a few words to her, and we will join you later on.

Lady Hunstanton: Ah, of course, You will have a great deal to say to her, and she will have a great deal to thank you for. It is not every son who gets such an offer, Mrs. Arbuthnot. But I know you appreciate that, dear.

Lady Caroline: John!

Lady Hunstanton: Now, don't keep Mrs. Arbuthnot too long, Lord Illingworth. We can't spare her.

Exit following the other guests. Sound of violin heard from music-room.

Lord Illingworth: So that is our son, Rachel! Well, I am very proud of him. He is a Harford, every inch of him. By the way, why Arbuthnot, Rachel?

Mrs. Arbuthnot: One name is as good as another, when one has no right to any name.

Lord Illingworth: I suppose so – but why Gerald?

Mrs. Arbuthnot: After a man whose heart I broke – after my father.

Lord Illingworth: Well, Rachel, what is over is over. All I have got to say now is that I am very, very much pleased with our boy. The world will know him merely as my private secretary, but to me he will be something very near, and very dear. It is a curious thing, Rachel; my life seemed to be quite complete. It was not so. It lacked something, it lacked a son. I have found my son now, I am glad I have found him.

Mrs. Arbuthnot: You have no right to claim him, or the smallest part of him. The boy is entirely mine, and shall remain mine.

Lord Illingworth: My dear Rachel, you have had him to yourself for over twenty years. Why not let me have him for a little now? He is quite as much mine as yours.

Mrs. Arbuthnot: Are you talking of the child you abandoned? Of the child who, as far as you are concerned, might have died of hunger and of want?

Lord Illingworth: You forget, Rachel, it was you who left me. It was not I who left you.

Mrs. Arbuthnot: I left you because you refused to give the child a name. Before my son was born, I implored you to marry me.

Lord Illingworth: I had no expectations then. And besides, Rachel, I wasn't much older than you were. I was only twenty-two. I was twenty-one, I believe, when the whole thing began in your father's garden.

Mrs. Arbuthnot: When a man is old enough to do wrong he should be old enough to do right also.

Lord Illingworth: My dear Rachel, intellectual generalities are always interesting, but generalities in morals mean absolutely nothing. As for saying I left our child to starve, that, of course, is untrue and silly. My mother offered you six hundred a year. But you wouldn't take anything. You simply disappeared, and carried the child away with you.

Mrs. Arbuthnot: I wouldn't have accepted a penny from her. Your father was different. He told you, in my presence, when we were in Paris, that it was your duty to marry me.

Lord Illingworth: Oh, duty is what one expects from others, it is not what one does oneself. Of course, I was influenced by my mother. Every man is when he is young.

Mrs. Arbuthnot: I am glad to hear you say so. Gerald shall certainly not go away with you.

Lord Illingworth: What nonsense, Rachel!

Mrs. Arbuthnot: Do you think I would allow my son –

Lord Illingworth: Our son.

Mrs. Arbuthnot: My son – (LORD ILLINGWORTH *shrugs his shoulders*) – to go away with the man who spoiled my youth, who ruined my life, who has tainted every moment of my days? You don't realise what my past has been in suffering and in shame.

Lord Illingworth: My dear Rachel, I must candidly say that I think Gerald's future considerably more important than your past.

Mrs. Arbuthnot: Gerald cannot separate his future from my past.

Lord Illingworth: That is exactly what he should do. That is exactly what you should help him to do. What a typical woman you are! You talk sentimentally, and you are thoroughly selfish the whole time. But don't let us have a scene. Rachel, I want you to look at this matter from the common-sense point of view, from the point of view of what is best for our son, leaving you and me out of the question. What is our son at present? An underpaid clerk in a small Provincial Bank in a third-rate English town. If you imagine he is quite happy in such a position, you are mistaken. He is thoroughly discontented.

Mrs. Arbuthnot: He was not discontented till he met you. You have made him so.

Lord Illingworth: Of course, I made him so. Discontent is the first step in the progress of a man or a nation. But I did not leave him with a mere longing for things he could not get. No, I made him a charming offer. He jumped at it, I need hardly say. Any young man would. And now, simply because it turns out that I am the boy's own father and he my own son, you propose practically to ruin his career. That is to say, if I were a perfect stranger, you would allow Gerald to go away with me, but as he is my own flesh and blood you won't. How utterly illogical you are!

Mrs. Arbuthnot: I will not allow him to go.

Lord Illingworth: How can you prevent it? What excuse can you give to him for making him decline such an offer as mine? I won't tell him in what relations I stand to him, I need hardly say. But you daren't tell him. You know that. Look how you have brought him up.

Mrs. Arbuthnot: I have brought him up to be a good man.

Lord Illingworth: Quite so. And what is the result? You have educated him to be your judge if he ever finds you out. And a bitter, an unjust judge he will be to you. Don't be deceived, Rachel. Children begin by loving their parents. After a time they judge them. Rarely, if ever, do they forgive them.

Mrs. Arbuthnot: George, don't take my son away from me. I have had twenty years of sorrow, and I have only had one thing to love me, only one thing to love. You have had a life of joy, and pleasure, and success. You have been quite happy, you have never thought of us. There was no reason, according to your views of life, why you should have remembered us at all. Your meeting us was a mere accident, a horrible accident. Forget it. Don't come now, and rob me of – of all I have in the whole world. You are so rich in other things. Leave me the little vineyard of my life; leave me the walled-in garden and the well of water; the ewe-lamb God sent me, in pity or in wrath, oh! leave me that. George, don't take Gerald from me.

Lord Illingworth: Rachel, at the present moment you are not necessary to Gerald's career; I am. There is nothing more to be said on the subject.

Mrs. Arbuthnot: I will not let him go.

Lord Illingworth: Here is Gerald. He has a right to decide for himself.

Enter GERALD.

Gerald: Well, dear mother, I hope you have settled it all with Lord Illingworth?

Mrs. Arbuthnot: I have not, Gerald.

Lord Illingworth: Your mother seems not to like your coming with me, for some reason.

Gerald: Why, mother?

Mrs. Arbuthnot: I thought you were quite happy here with me, Gerald. I didn't know you were so anxious to leave me.

Gerald: Mother, how can you talk like that? Of course I have been quite happy with you. But a man can't stay always with his mother. No chap does. I want to make myself a position, to do something. I thought you would have been proud to see me Lord Illingworth's secretary.

Mrs. Arbuthnot: I do not think you would be suitable as a private secretary to Lord Illingworth. You have no qualifications.

Lord Illingworth: I don't wish to seem to interfere for a moment, Mrs. Arbuthnot, but as far as your last objection is concerned, I surely am the best judge. And I can only tell you that your son has all the qualifications I had hoped for. He has more, in fact, than I had even thought of. Far more. (MRS. ARBUTHNOT *remains silent.*) Have you any other reason, Mrs. Arbuthnot, why you don't wish your son to accept this post?

Gerald: Have you, mother? Do answer.

Lord Illingworth: If you have, Mrs. Arbuthnot, pray, pray say it. We are quite by ourselves here. Whatever it is, I need not say I will not repeat it.

Gerald: Mother?

Lord Illingworth: If you would like to be alone with your son, I will leave you. You may have some other reason you don't wish me to hear.

Mrs. Arbuthnot: I have no other reason.

Lord Illingworth: Then, my dear boy, we may look on the thing as settled. Come, you and I will smoke a cigarette on the terrace together. And Mrs. Arbuthnot, pray let me tell you, that I think you have acted very, very wisely.

Exit with GERALD. MRS. ARBUTHNOT *is left alone. She stands immobile with a look of unutterable sorrow on her face.*

ACT DROP.

THIRD ACT

SCENE

The picture gallery at Hunstanton. Door at back leading on to terrace.
LORD ILLINGWORTH *and* GERALD, *R.C.* LORD
ILLINGWORTH *lolling on a sofa.* GERALD *in a chair.*

Lord Illingworth: Thoroughly sensible woman, your mother,
Gerald. I knew she would come round in the end.

Gerald: My mother is awfully conscientious, Lord Illingworth,
and I know she doesn't think I am educated enough to be your secretary. She is perfectly right, too. I was fearfully idle when I was at
school, and I couldn't pass an examination now to save my life.

Lord Illingworth: My dear Gerald, examinations are of no value
whatsoever. If a man is a gentleman, he knows quite enough, and if
he is not a gentleman, whatever he knows is bad for him.

Gerald: But I am so ignorant of the world, Lord Illingworth.

Lord Illingworth: Don't be afraid, Gerald. Remember that you've
got on your side the most wonderful thing in the world – youth!
There is nothing like youth. The middle-aged are mortgaged to
Life. The old are in life's lumber-room. But youth is the Lord of
Life. Youth has a kingdom waiting for it. Every one is born a king,
and most people die in exile like most kings. To win back my youth,
Gerald, there is nothing I wouldn't do – except take exercise, get up
early, or be a useful member of the community.

Gerald: But you don't call yourself old, Lord Illingworth?

Lord Illingworth: I am old enough to be your father, Gerald.

Gerald: I don't remember my father; he died years ago.

Lord Illingworth: So Lady Hunstanton told me.

Gerald: It is very curious, my mother never talks to me about my
father. I sometimes think she must have married beneath her.

Lord Illingworth (winces slightly): Really? (*Goes over and puts his
hand on* GERALD'S *shoulder.*) You have missed not having a father,
I suppose, Gerald?

Gerald: Oh, no; my mother has been so good to me. No one ever
had such a mother as I have had.

Lord Illingworth: I am quite sure of that. Still I should imagine that most mothers don't quite understand their sons. Don't realise, I mean, that a son has ambitions, a desire to see life, to make himself a name. After all, Gerald, you couldn't be expected to pass all your life in such a hole as Wrockley, could you?

Gerald: Oh, no! It would be dreadful!

Lord Illingworth: A mother's love is very touching of course, but it is often curiously selfish. I mean there is a good deal of selfishness in it.

Gerald (slowly): I suppose there is.

Lord Illingworth: Your mother is a thoroughly good woman. But good women have such limited views of life, their horizon is so small, their interests are so petty, aren't they?

Gerald: They are awfully interested, certainly, in things we don't care much about.

Lord Illingworth: I suppose your mother is very religious, and that sort of thing.

Gerald: Oh, yes, she's always going to church.

Lord Illingworth: Ah! she is not modern, and to be modern is the only thing worth being nowadays. You want to be modern, don't you, Gerald? You want to know life as it really is. Not to be put off with any old-fashioned theories about life. Well, what you have to do at present is simply to fit yourself for the best society. A man who can dominate a London dinner-table can dominate the world. The future belongs to the dandy. It is the exquisites who are going to rule.

Gerald: I should like to wear nice things awfully, but I have always been told that a man should not think so much about his clothes.

Lord Illingworth: People nowadays are so absolutely superficial that they don't understand the philosophy of the superficial. By the way, Gerald, you should learn how to tie your tie better. Sentiment is all very well for the button-hole. But the essential thing for a necktie is style. A well-tied tie is the first serious step in life.

Gerald (laughing): I might be able to learn how to tie a tie, Lord Illingworth, but I should never be able to talk as you do. I don't know how to talk.

Lord Illingworth: Oh! talk to every woman as if you loved her, and to every man as if he bored you, and at the end of your first season you will have the reputation of possessing the most perfect social tact.

Gerald: But it is very difficult to get into society, isn't it?

Lord Illingworth: To get into the best society, nowadays, one has either to feed people, amuse people, or shock people – that is all!

Gerald: I suppose society is wonderfully delightful!

Lord Illingworth: To be in it is merely a bore. But to be out of it simply a tragedy. Society is a necessary thing. No man has any real success in this world unless he has got women to back him, and women rule society. If you have not got women on your side you are quite over. You might just as well be a barrister or a stock-broker, or a journalist at once.

Gerald: It is very difficult to understand women is it not?

Lord Illingworth: You should never try to understand them. Women are pictures. Men are problems. If you want to know what a woman really means – which, by the way, is always a dangerous thing to do – look at her, don't listen to her.

Gerald: But women are awfully clever, aren't they?

Lord Illingworth: One should always tell them so. But, to the philosopher, my dear Gerald, women represent the triumph of matter over mind – just as men represent the triumph of mind over morals.

Gerald: How then can women have so much power as you say they have?

Lord Illingworth: The history of women is the history of the worst form of tyranny the world has ever known. The tyranny of the weak over the strong. It is the only tyranny that lasts.

Gerald: But haven't women got a refining influence?

Lord Illingworth: Nothing refines but the intellect.

Gerald: Still, there are many different kinds of women, aren't there?

Lord Illingworth: Only two kinds in society: the plain and the coloured.

Gerald: But there are good women in society, aren't there?

Lord Illingworth: Far too many.

Gerald: But do you think women shouldn't be good?

Lord Illingworth: One should never tell them so, they'd all become good at once. Women are a fascinatingly wilful sex. Every woman is a rebel, and usually in wild revolt against herself.

Gerald: You have never been married, Lord Illingworth, have you?

Lord Illingworth: Men marry because they are tired; women because they are curious. Both are disappointed.

Gerald: But don't you think one can be happy when one is married?

Lord Illingworth: Perfectly happy. But the happiness of a married man, my dear Gerald, depends on the people he has not married.

Gerald: But if one is in love?

Lord Illingworth: One should always be in love. That is the reason one should never marry.

Gerald: Love is a very wonderful thing, isn't it?

Lord Illingworth: When one is in love one begins by deceiving oneself. And one ends by deceiving others. That is what the world calls a romance. But a really *grande passion* is comparatively rare nowadays. It is the privilege of people who have nothing to do. That is the one use of the idle classes in a country, and the only possible explanation of us Harfords.

Gerald: Harfords, Lord Illingworth?

Lord Illingworth: That is my family name. You should study the Peerage, Gerald. It is the one book a young man about town should know thoroughly, and it is the best thing in fiction the English have ever done. And now, Gerald, you are going into a perfectly new life with me, and I want you to know how to live.

MRS. ARBUTHNOT *appears on terrace behind.*

For the world has been made by fools that wise men should live in it!

Enter L.C. LADY HUNSTANTON *and* DR. DAUBENY.

Lady Hunstanton: Ah! here you are, dear Lord Illingworth. Well, I suppose you have been telling our young friend, Gerald, what his new duties are to be, and giving him a great deal of good advice over a pleasant cigarette.

Lord Illingworth: I have been giving him the best of advice, Lady Hunstanton, and the best of cigarettes.

Lady Hunstanton: I am so sorry I was not here to listen to you, but I suppose I am too old now to learn. Except from you, dear Archdeacon, when you are in your nice pulpit. But then I always know what you are going to say, so I don't feel alarmed. (*Sees* MRS. ARBUTHNOT.) Ah! dear Mrs. Arbuthnot, do come and join us. Come, dear.

Enter MRS. ARBUTHNOT.

Gerald has been having such a long talk with Lord Illingworth; I am sure you must feel very much flattered at the pleasant way in which everything has turned out for him. Let us sit down. (*They sit down.*) And how is your beautiful embroidery going on?

Mrs. Arbuthnot: I am always at work, Lady Hunstanton.

Lady Hunstanton: Mrs. Daubeny embroiders a little, too, doesn't she?

The Archdeacon: She was very deft with her needle once, quite a Dorcas. But the gout has crippled her fingers a good deal. She has not touched the tambour frame for nine or ten years. But she has many other amusements. She is very much interested in her own health.

Lady Hunstanton: Ah! that is always a nice distraction, is it not? Now, what are you talking about, Lord Illingworth? Do tell us.

Lord Illingworth: I was on the point of explaining to Gerald that the world has always laughed at its own tragedies, that being the only way in which it has been able to bear them. And that, consequently, whatever the world has treated seriously belongs to the comedy side of things.

Lady Hunstanton: Now I am quite out of my depth. I usually am when Lord Illingworth says anything. And the Humane Society is most careless. They never rescue me. I am left to sink. I have a dim idea, dear Lord Illingworth, that you are always on the side of the sinners, and I know I always try to be on the side of the saints, but that is as far as I get. And after all, it may be merely the fancy of a drowning person.

Lord Illingworth: The only difference between the saint and the sinner is that every saint has a past, and every sinner has a future.

Lady Hunstanton: Ah! that quite does for me. I haven't a word to say. You and I, dear Mrs. Arbuthnot, are behind the age. We can't follow Lord Illingworth. Too much care was taken with our education, I am afraid. To have been well brought up is a great drawback nowadays. It shuts one out from so much.

Mrs. Arbuthnot: I should be sorry to follow Lord Illingworth in any of his opinions.

Lady Hunstanton: You are quite right, dear.

GERALD *shrugs his shoulders and looks irritably over at his mother.* *Enter* LADY CAROLINE.

Lady Caroline: Jane, have you seen John anywhere?

Lady Hunstanton: You needn't be anxious about him, dear. He is with Lady Stutfield; I saw them some time ago, in the Yellow Drawing-room. They seem quite happy together. You are not going, Caroline? Pray sit down.

Lady Caroline: I think I had better look after John.

Exit LADY CAROLINE.

Lady Hunstanton: It doesn't do to pay men so much attention. And Caroline has really nothing to be anxious about. Lady Stutfield is very sympathetic. She is just as sympathetic about one thing as she is about another. A beautiful nature.

Enter SIR JOHN *and* MRS ALLONBY.

Ah! here is Sir John! And with Mrs. Allonby too! I suppose it was Mrs. Allonby I saw him with. Sir John, Caroline has been looking everywhere for you.

Mrs. Allonby: We have been waiting for her in the Music-room, dear Lady Hunstanton.

Lady Hunstanton: Ah! the Music-room, of course. I thought it was the Yellow Drawing-room, my memory is getting so defective. (*To the* ARCHDEACON.) Mrs. Daubeny has a wonderful memory, hasn't she?

The Archdeacon: She used to be quite remarkable for her memory, but since her last attack she recalls chiefly the events of her early childhood. But she finds great pleasure in such retrospections, great pleasure.

Enter LADY STUTFIELD *and* MR. KELVIL.

Lady Hunstanton: Ah! dear Lady Stutfield! and what has Mr. Kelvil been talking to you about?

Lady Stutfield: About Bimetallism, as well as I remember.

Lady Hunstanton: Bimetallism! Is that quite a nice subject? However, I know people discuss everything very freely nowadays. What did Sir John talk to you about, dear Mrs. Allonby?

Mrs. Allonby: About Patagonia.

Lady Hunstanton: Really? What a remote topic! But very improving, I have no doubt.

Mrs. Allonby: He has been most interesting on the subject of Patagonia. Savages seem to have quite the same views as cultured people on almost all subjects. They are excessively advanced.

Lady Hunstanton: What do they do?

Mrs. Allonby: Apparently everything.

Lady Hunstanton: Well, it is very gratifying, dear Archdeacon, is it not, to find that Human Nature is permanently one. – On the whole, the world is the same world, is it not?

Lord Illingworth: The world is simply divided into two classes – those who believe the incredible, like the public – and those who do the improbable –

Mrs. Allonby: Like yourself?

Lord Illingworth: Yes; I am always astonishing myself. It is the only thing that makes life worth living.

Lady Stutfield: And what have you been doing lately that astonishes you?

Lord Illingworth: I have been discovering all kinds of beautiful qualities in my own nature.

Mrs. Allonby: Ah! don't become quite perfect all at once. Do it gradually!

Lord Illingworth: I don't intend to grow perfect at all. At least, I hope I shan't. It would be most inconvenient. Women love us for our defects. If we have enough of them, they will forgive us everything, even our gigantic intellects.

Mrs. Allonby: It is premature to ask us to forgive analysis. We forgive adoration; that is quite as much as should be expected from us.

Enter LORD ALFRED. *He joins* LADY STUTFIELD.

Lady Hunstanton: Ah! we women should forgive everything, shouldn't we, dear Mrs. Arbuthnot? I am sure you agree with me in that.

Mrs. Arbuthnot: I do not, Lady Hunstanton. I think there are many things women should never forgive.

Lady Hunstanton: What sort of things?

Mrs. Arbuthnot: The ruin of another woman's life. (*Moves slowly away to back of stage.*)

Lady Hunstanton: Ah! those things are very sad, no doubt, but I believe there are admirable homes where people of that kind are looked after and reformed, and I think on the whole that the secret of life is to take things very, very easily.

Mrs. Allonby: The secret of life is never to have an emotion that is unbecoming.

Lady Stutfield: The secret of life is to appreciate the pleasure of being terribly, terribly deceived.

Kelvil: The secret of life is to resist temptation, Lady Stutfield.

Lord Illingworth: There is no secret of life. Life's aim, if it has one, is simply to be always looking for temptations. There are not nearly enough. I sometimes pass a whole day without coming across a single one. It is quite dreadful. It makes one so nervous about the future.

Lady Hunstanton (*shakes her fan at him*): I don't know how it is, dear Lord Illingworth, but everything you have said to-day seems to me excessively immoral. It has been most interesting, listening to you.

Lord Illingworth: All thought is immoral. Its very essence is destruction. If you think of anything, you kill it. Nothing survives being thought of.

Lady Hunstanton: I don't understand a word, Lord Illingworth. But I have no doubt it is all quite true. Personally, I have very little to reproach myself with, on the score of thinking. I don't believe in women thinking too much. Women should think in moderation, as they should do all things in moderation.

Lord Illingworth: Moderation is a fatal thing, Lady Hunstanton. Nothing succeeds like excess.

Lady Hunstanton: I hope I shall remember that. It sounds an admirable maxim. But I'm beginning to forget everything. It's a great misfortune.

Lord Illingworth: It is one of your most fascinating qualities, Lady Hunstanton. No woman should have a memory. Memory in a woman is the beginning of dowdiness. One can always tell from a woman's bonnet whether she has got a memory or not.

Lady Hutnstanton: How charming you are, dear *Lord Illingworth*. You always find out that one's most glaring fault is one's most important virtue. You have the most comforting view of life.

Enter FARQUHAR

Farquhar: Doctor Daubeny's carriage!

Lady Hunstanton: My dear Archdeacon! It is only half-past ten.

The Archdeacon (*rising*): I am afraid I must go, Lady Hunstanton. Tuesday is always one of Mrs. Daubeny's bad nights.

Lady Hunstanton (*rising*): Well, I won't keep you from her. (*Goes with him towards door.*) I have told Farquhar to put a brace of partridge into the carriage. Mrs. Daubeny may fancy them.

The Archdeacon: It is very kind of you, but Mrs. Daubeny never touches solids now. Lives entirely on jellies. But she is wonderfully cheerful, wonderfully cheerful. She has nothing to complain of.

Exit with LADY HUNSTANTON.

Mrs. Allonby (*goes over to Lord Illingworth.*) There is a beautiful moon to-night.

Lord Illingworth: Let us go and look at it. To look at anything that is inconstant is charming nowadays.

Mrs. Allonby: You have your looking-glass.

Lord Illingworth: It is unkind. It merely shows me my wrinkles.

Mrs. Allonby: Mine is better behaved. It never tells me the truth.

Lord Illingworth: Then it is in love with you.

Exeunt SIR JOHN, LADY STUTFIELD, MR. KELVIL, *and* LORD ALFRED.

Gerald (*to Lord Illingworth*): May I come too?

Lord Illingworth: Do, my dear boy. (*Moves towards door with* MRS. ALLONBY *and* GERALD.)

LADY CAROLINE *enters, looks rapidly round and goes out in opposite direction to that taken by* JOHN *and* LADY STUTFIELD.

Mrs. Arbuthnot: Gerald!

Gerald: What, mother!

Exit LORD ILLINGWORTH *with* MRS. ALLONBY.

Mrs. Arbuthnot: It is getting late. Let us go home.

Gerald: My dear mother. Do let us wait a little longer. Lord Illingworth is so delightful, and, by the way, mother, I have a great surprise for you. We are starting for India at the end of this month.

Mrs. Arbuthnot: Let us go home.

Gerald: If you really want to, of course, mother, but I must bid good-bye to Lord Illingworth first. I'll be back in five minutes. (*Exit.*)

Mrs. Arbuthnot: Let him leave me if he chooses, but not with him – not with him! I couldn't bear it. (*Walks up and down.*)

Enter HESTER.

Hester: What a lovely night it is, Mrs. Arbuthnot.

Mrs. Arbuthnot: Is it?

Hester: Mrs. Arbuthnot, I wish you would let us be friends. You are so different from the other women here. When you came into the Drawing-room this evening, somehow you brought with you a sense of what is good and pure in life. I had been foolish. There are things that are right to say, but that may be said at the wrong time and to the wrong people.

Mrs. Arbuthnot: I heard what you said. I agree with it, Miss Worsley.

Hester: I didn't know you had heard it. But I knew you would agree with me. A woman who has sinned should be punished, shouldn't she?

Mrs. Arbuthnot: Yes.

Hester: She shouldn't be allowed to come into the society of good men and women?

Mrs. Arbuthnot: She should not.

Hester: And the man should be punished in the same way?

Mrs. Arbuthnot: In the same way. And the children, if there are children, in the same way also?

Hester: Yes, it is right that the sins of the parents should be visited on the children. It is a just law. It is God's law.

Mrs. Arbuthnot: It is one of God's terrible laws. (*Moves away to fireplace.*)

Hester: You are distressed about your son leaving you, Mrs. Arbuthnot?

Mrs. Arbuthnot: Yes.

Hester: Do you like him going away with Lord Illingworth? Of course there is position, no doubt, and money, but position and money are not everything, are they?

Mrs. Arbuthnot: They are nothing; they bring misery.

Hester: Then why do you let your son go with him?

Mrs. Arbuthnot: He wishes it himself.

Hester: But if you asked him he would stay, would he not?

Mrs. Arbuthnot: He has set his heart on going.

Hester: He couldn't refuse you anything. He loves you too much. Ask him to stay. Let me send him to you. He is on the terrace at this moment with Lord Illingworth. I heard them laughing together as I passed through the Music-room.

Mrs. Arbuthnot: Don't trouble, Miss Worsley, I can wait. It is of no consequence.

Hester: No, I'll tell him you want him. Do – do ask him to stay.

Exit HESTER.

Mrs. Arbuthnot: He won't come – I know he won't come.

Enter LADY CAROLINE. *She looks round anxiously. Enter* GERALD.

Lady Caroline: Mr. Arbuthnot, may I ask you is Sir John anywhere on the terrace?

Gerald: No, Lady Caroline, he is not on the terrace.

Lady Caroline: It is very curious. It is time for him to retire.

Exit LADY CAROLINE.

Gerald: Dear mother, I am afraid I kept you waiting. I forgot all about it. I am so happy to-night, mother; I have never been so happy.

Mrs. Arbuthnot: At the prospect of going away?

Gerald: Don't put it like that, mother. Of course I am sorry to leave you. Why, you are the best mother in the whole world. But after all, as Lord Illingworth says, it is impossible to live in such a place as Wrockley. You don't mind it. But I'm ambitious; I want something more than that. I want to have a career. I want to do something that will make you proud of me, and Lord Illingworth is going to help me. He is going to do everything for me.

Mrs. Arbuthnot: Gerald, don't go away with Lord Illingworth. I implore you not to. Gerald, I beg you!

Gerald: Mother, how changeable you are! You don't seem to know your own mind for a single moment. An hour and a half ago in the Drawing-room you agreed to the whole thing; now you turn round and make objections, and try to force me to give up my one chance in life. Yes, my one chance. You don't suppose that men like Lord Illingworth are to be found every day, do you, mother? It is very strange that when I have had such a wonderful piece of good luck, the one person to put difficulties in my way should be my own mother. Besides, you know, mother, I love Hester Worsley. Who could help loving her? I love her more than I have ever told you, far more. And if I had a position, if I had prospects, I could – I could ask her to. . . . Don't you understand now, mother, what it means to me to be Lord Illingworth's secretary? To start like that is to find a career ready for one – before one – waiting for one. If I were Lord Illingworth's secretary I could ask Hester to be my wife. As a wretched bank clerk with a hundred a year it would be an impertinence.

Mrs. Arbuthnot: I fear you need have no hopes of Miss Worsley. I know her views on life. She has just told them to me. (*A pause.*)

Gerald: Then I have my ambition left, at any rate. That is something – I am glad I have that! You have always tried to crush my ambition, mother – haven't you? You have told me that the world is a wicked place, that success is not worth having, that society is shallow, and all that sort of thing – well, I don't believe it, mother. I think the world must be delightful. I think society must be exquisite. I think success is a thing worth having. You have been wrong in all that you taught me, mother, quite wrong. Lord Illingworth is a successful man. He is a fashionable man. He is a man who lives in the world and for it. Well, I would give anything to be just like Lord Illingworth.

Mrs. Arbuthnot: I would sooner see you dead.

Gerald: Mother, what is your objection to Lord Illingworth? Tell me – tell me right out. What is it?

Mrs. Arbuthnot: He is a bad man.

Gerald: In what way bad? I don't understand what you mean.

Mrs. Arbuthnot: I will tell you.

Gerald: I suppose you think him bad, because he doesn't believe the same things as you do. Well, men are different from women, mother. It is natural that they should have different views.

Mrs. Arbuthnot: It is not what Lord Illingworth believes, or what he does not believe, that makes him bad. It is what he is.

Gerald: Mother, is it something you know of him? Something you actually know?

Mrs. Arbuthnot: It is something I know.

Gerald: Something you are quite sure of?

Mrs. Arbuthnot: Quite sure of.

Gerald: How long have you known it?

Mrs. Arbuthnot: For twenty years.

Gerald: Is it fair to go back twenty years in any man's career? And what have you or I to do with Lord Illingworth's early life? What business is it of ours?

Mrs. Arbuthnot: What this man has been, he is now, and will be always.

Gerald: Mother, tell me what Lord Illingworth did? If he did anything shameful, I will not go away with him. Surely you know me well enough for that?

Mrs. Arbuthnot: Gerald, come near to me. Quite close to me, as you used to do when you were a little boy, when you were mother's own boy.

GERALD *sits down beside his mother. She runs her fingers through his hair, and strokes his hands.*

Gerald, there was a girl once, she was very young, she was little over eighteen at the time. George Harford – that was Lord Illingworth's name then – George Harford met her. She knew nothing about life. He – knew everything. He made this girl love him. He made her love so much that she left her father's house with him one morning. She loved him so much, and he had promised to marry her! He had solemnly promised to marry her, and she had believed him. She was very young, and – and ignorant of what life really is. But he put the marriage off from week to week, and month to month. – She trusted in him all the while. She loved him. – Before her child was born – for she had a child – she implored him for the child's sake to marry her, that the child might have a name, that her sin might not be visited on the child, who was innocent. He refused. After the child was born she left him, taking the child away, and her life was ruined, and her soul ruined, and all that was sweet, and good, and pure in her ruined also. She suffered terribly – she suffers now. She will always suffer. For her there is no joy, no peace, no atonement. She is a woman who drags a chain like a guilty thing. She is a woman who wears a mask, like a thing that is a leper. The fire cannot purify her. The waters cannot quench her anguish. Nothing can heal her! no anodyne can give her sleep! no poppies forgetfulness! She is lost! She is a lost soul! – That is why I call Lord Illingworth a bad man. That is why I don't want my boy to be with him.

Gerald: My dear mother, it all sounds very tragic, of course. But I dare say the girl was just as much to blame as Lord Illingworth was. – After all, would a really nice girl, a girl with any nice feelings at all, go away from her home with a man to whom she was not married, and live with him as his wife? No nice girl would.

Mrs. Arbuthnot (after a pause): Gerald, I withdraw all my objections. You are at liberty to go away with Lord Illingworth, when and where you choose.

Gerald: Dear mother, I knew you wouldn't stand in my way. You are the best woman God ever made. And, as for Lord Illingworth, I don't believe he is capable of anything infamous or base. I can't believe it of him – I can't.

Hester (outside): Let me go! Let me go!

Enter HESTER *in terror, and rushes over to* GERALD *and flings herself in his arms.*

Hester: Oh! save me – save me from him!
Gerald: From whom?
Hester: He has insulted me! Horribly insulted me! Save me!

Gerald: Who? Who has dared?

LORD ILLINGWORTH *enters at back of stage.* HESTER *breaks from* GERALD'S *arms and points to him.*

Gerald (he is quite beside himself with rage and indignation): Lord Illingworth, you have insulted the purest thing on God's earth, a thing as pure as my own mother. You have insulted the woman I love most in the world with my own mother. As there is a God in Heaven, I will kill you!

Mrs. Arbuthnot (rushing across and catching hold of him): No! no!

Gerald (thrusting her back): Don't hold me, mother. Don't hold me – I'll kill him!

Mrs. Arbuthnot: Gerald!

Gerald: Let me go, I say!

Mrs. Arbuthnot: Stop, Gerald, stop! He is your own father!

GERALD *clutches his mother's hands and looks into her face. She sinks slowly on the ground in shame.* HESTER *steals towards the door.* LORD ILLINGWORTH *frowns and bites his lip. After a time,* GERALD *raises his mother up, puts his arm round her, and leads her from the room.*

ACT DROP.

FOURTH ACT

SCENE

Sitting-room at Mrs. Arbuthnot's. Large open French window at back, looking on to garden. Doors R.C. and L.C.

GERALD ARBUTHNOT *writing at table.*
Enter ALICE *R.C. followed by* LADY HUNSTANTON *and* MRS. ALLONBY.

Alice: Lady Hunstanton and Mrs. Allonby.(*Exit L.C.*)

Lady Hunstanton: Good-morning, Gerald.

Gerald (rising): Good-morning, Lady Hunstanton. Good-morning, Mrs. Allonby.

Lady Hunstanton (sitting down): We came to inquire for your dear mother, Gerald. I hope she is better?

Gerald: My mother has not come down yet, Lady Hunstanton.

Lady Hunstanton: Ah, I am afraid the heat was too much for her last night. I think there must have been thunder in the air. Or perhaps it was the music. Music makes one feel so romantic – at least it always gets on one's nerves.

Mrs. Allonby: It's the same thing, nowadays.

Lady Hunstanton: I am so glad I don't know what you mean, dear. I am afraid you mean something wrong. Ah, I see you're examining Mrs. Arbuthnot's pretty room. Isn't it nice and old-fashioned?

Mrs. Allonby (surveying the room through her lorgnette): It looks quite the happy English home.

Lady Hunstanton: That's just the word, dear; that just describes it. One feels your mother's good influence in everything she has about her, Gerald.

Mrs. Allonby: Lord Illingworth says that all influence is bad, but that a good influence is the worst in the world.

Lady Hunstanton: When Lord Illingworth knows Mrs. Arbuthnot better he will change his mind. I must certainly bring him here.

Mrs. Allonby: I should like to see Lord Illingworth in a happy English home.

Lady Hunstanton: It would do him a great deal of good, dear.

Most women in London, nowadays, seem to furnish their rooms with nothing but orchids, foreigners, and French novels. But here we have the room of a sweet saint. Fresh natural flowers, books that don't shock one, pictures that one can look at without blushing.

Mrs. Allonby: But I like blushing.

Lady Hunstanton: Well, there is a good deal to be said for blushing, if one can do it at the proper moment. Poor dear Hunstanton used to tell me I didn't blush nearly often enough. But then he was so very particular. He wouldn't let me know any of his men friends, except those who were over seventy, like poor Lord Ashton; who afterwards, by the way, was brought into the Divorce Court. A most unfortunate case.

Mrs. Allonby: I delight in men over seventy. They always offer one the devotion of a lifetime. I think seventy an ideal age for a man.

Lady Hunstanton: She is quite incorrigible, Gerald, isn't she? By-the-by, Gerald, I hope your dear mother will come and see me more often now. You and Lord Illingworth start almost immediately, don't you?

Gerald: I have given up my intention of being Lord Illingworth's secretary.

Lady Hunstanton: Surely not, Gerald! It would be most unwise of you. What reason can you have?

Gerald: I don't think I should be suitable for the post.

Mrs. Allonby: I wish Lord Illingworth would ask me to be his secretary. But he says I am not serious enough.

Lady Hunstanton: My dear, you really mustn't talk like that in this house. Mrs. Arbuthnot doesn't know anything about the wicked society in which we all live. She won't go into it. She is far too good. I consider it was a great honour her coming to me last night. It gave quite an atmosphere of respectability to the party.

Mrs. Allonby: Ah, that must have been what you thought was thunder in the air.

Lady Hunstanton: My dear, how can you say that? There is no resemblance between the two things at all. But really, Gerald, what do you mean by not being suitable?

Gerald: Lord Illingworth's views of life and mine are too different.

Lady Hunstanton: But, my dear Gerald, at your age you shouldn't have any views of life. They are quite out of place. You must be guided by others in this matter. Lord Illingworth has made you the most flattering offer, and travelling with him you would see the world – as much of it, at least, as one should look at – under the best auspices possible, and stay with all the right people, which is so important at this solemn moment in your career.

Gerald: I don't want to see the world, I've seen enough of it.

Mrs. Allonby: I hope you don't think you have exhausted life, Mr. Arbuthnot. When a man says that, one knows that life has exhausted him.

Gerald: I don't wish to leave my mother.

Lady Hunstanton: Now, Gerald, that is pure laziness on your part. Not leave your mother! If I were your mother I would insist on your going.

Enter ALICE *L.C.*

Alice: Mrs. Arbuthnot's compliments, my lady, but she has a bad headache, and cannot see any one this morning. (*Exit R.C.*)

Lady Hunstanton (*rising*): A bad headache! I am so sorry! Perhaps you'll bring her up to Hunstanton this afternoon, if she is better, Gerald.

Gerald: I am afraid not this afternoon, Lady Hunstanton.

Lady Hunstanton: Well, to-morrow, then. Ah, if you had a father, Gerald, he wouldn't let you waste your life here. He would send you off with Lord Illingworth at once. But mothers are so weak. They give up to their sons in everything. We are all heart, all heart. Come, dear, I must call at the rectory and inquire for Mrs. Daubeny, who, I am afraid, is far from well. It is wonderful how the Archdeacon bears up, quite wonderful. He is the most sympathetic of husbands. Quite a model. Good-bye, Gerald, give my fondest love to your mother

Mrs. Allonby: Good-bye, Mr. Arbuthnot.

Gerald: Good-bye.

Exit LADY HUNSTANTON *and* MRS. ALLONBY. GERALD *sits down and reads over his letter.*

Gerald: What name can I sign? I, who have no right to any name. (*Signs name, puts letter into envelope, addresses it, and is about to seal it, when door L.C. opens and* MRS. ARBUTHNOT *enters.* GERALD *lays down sealing-wax. Mother and son look at each other.*)

Lady Hunstanton (*through French window at the back*): Good-bye again, Gerald. We are taking the short cut across your pretty garden. Now, remember my advice to you – start at once with Lord Illingworth.

Mrs. Allonby: Au revoir, Mr. Arbuthnot. Mind you bring me back something nice from your travels – not an Indian shawl – on no account an Indian shawl. (*Exeunt.*)

Gerald: Mother, I have just written to him.

Mrs. Arbuthnot: To whom?

Gerald: To my father. I have written to tell him to come here at four o'clock this afternoon.

Mrs. Arbuthnot: He shall not come here. He shall not cross the threshold of my house.

Gerald: He must come.

Mrs. Arbuthnot: Gerald, if you are going away with Lord Illingworth, go at once. Go before it kills me; but don't ask me to meet him.

Gerald: Mother, you don't understand. Nothing in the world would induce me to go away with Lord Illingworth, or to leave you. Surely you know me well enough for that. No, I have written to him to say –

Mrs. Arbuthnot: What can you have to say to him?

Gerald: Can't you guess, mother, what I have written in this letter?

Mrs. Arbuthnot: No.

Gerald: Mother, surely you can. Think, think what must be done, now, at once, within the next few days.

Mrs. Arbuthnot: There is nothing to be done.

Gerald: I have written to Lord Illingworth to tell him that he must marry you.

Mrs. Arbuthnot: Marry me?

Gerald: Mother, I will force him to do it. The wrong that has been done you must be repaired. Atonement must be made. Justice may be slow, mother, but it comes in the end. In a few days you shall be Lord Illingworth's lawful wife.

Mrs. Arbuthnot: But, Gerald –

Gerald: I will insist upon his doing it. I will make him do it, he will not dare to refuse.

Mrs. Arbuthnot: But, Gerald, it is I who refuse. I will not marry Lord Illingworth.

Gerald: Not marry him? Mother!

Mrs. Arbuthnot: I will not marry him.

Gerald: But you don't understand: it is for your sake I am talking, not for mine. This marriage, this necessary marriage, this marriage which for obvious reasons must inevitably take place, will not help me, will not give me a name that will be really, rightly mine to bear.

But surely it will be something for you, that you, my mother, should, however late, become the wife of the man who is my father. Will not that be something?

Mrs. Arbuthnot: I will not marry him.

Gerald: Mother, you must.

Mrs. Arbuthnot: I will not. You talk of atonement for a wrong done. What atonement can be made to me? There is no atonement possible. I am disgraced; he is not. That is all. It is the usual history of a man and a woman as it usually happens, as it always happens. And the ending is the ordinary ending. The woman suffers. The man goes free.

Gerald: I don't know if that is the ordinary ending, mother; I hope it is not. But your life, at any rate, shall not end like that. The man shall make whatever reparation is possible. It is not enough. It does not wipe out the past, I know that. But at least it makes the future better, better for you, mother.

Mrs. Arbuthnot: I refuse to marry Lord Illingworth.

Gerald: If he came to you himself and asked you to be his wife you would give him a different answer. Remember, he is my father.

Mrs. Arbuthnot: If he came himself, which he will not do, my answer would be the same. Remember I am your mother.

Gerald: Mother, you make it terribly difficult for me by talking like that; and I can't understand why you won't look at this matter from the right, from the only proper standpoint. It is to take away the bitterness out of your life, to take away the shadow that lies on your name, that this marriage must take place. There is no alternative; and after the marriage you and I can go away together. But the marriage must take place first. It is a duty that you owe, not merely to yourself, but to all other women – yes; to all the other women in the world, lest he betray more.

Mrs. Arbuthnot: I owe nothing to other women. There is not one of them to help me. There is not one woman in the world to whom I could go for pity, if I would take it, or for sympathy, if I could win it. Women are hard on each other. That girl, last night, good though she is, fled from the room as though I were a tainted thing. She was right. I am a tainted thing. But my wrongs are my own, and I will bear them alone. I must bear them alone. What have women who have not sinned to do witl me, or I with them? We do not understand each other.

Enter HESTER *behind.*

Gerald: I implore you to do what I ask you.

Mrs. Arbuthnot: What son has ever asked of his mother to make so hideous a sacrifice? None.

Gerald: What mother has ever refused to marry the father of her own child? None.

Mrs. Arbuthnot: Let me be the first, then. I will not do it.

Gerald: Mother, you believe in religion, and you brought me up to believe in it also. Well, surely your religion, the religion that you taught me when I was a boy, mother, must tell you that I am right. You know it, you feel it.

Mrs. Arbuthnot: I do not know it. I do not feel it, nor will I ever stand before God's altar and ask God's blessing on so hideous a mockery as a marriage between me and George Harford. I will not say the words the Church bids us to say. I will not say them. I dare not. How could I swear to love the man I loathe, to honour him who wrought you dishonour, to obey him who, in his mastery, made me to sin? No; marriage is a sacrament for those who love each other. It is not for such as him, or such as me. Gerald, to save you from the world's sneers and taunts I have lied to the world. For twenty years I have lied to the world. I could not tell the world the truth. Who can, ever? But not for my own sake will I lie to God, and in God's presence. No, Gerald, no ceremony, Church-hallowed or State-made, shall ever bind me to George Harford. It may be that I am too bound to him already, who, robbing me, yet left me richer, so that in the mire of my life I found the pearl of price, or what I thought would be so.

Gerald: I don't understand you now.

Mrs. Arbuthnot: Men don't understand what mothers are. I am no different from other women except in the wrong done me and the wrong I did, and my very heavy punishments and great disgrace. And yet, to bear you I had to look on death. To nurture you I had to wrestle with it. Death fought with me for you. All women have to fight with death to keep their children. Death, being childless, wants our children from us. Gerald, when you were naked I clothed you, when you were hungry I gave you food. Night and day all that long winter I tended you. No office is too mean, no care too lowly for the thing we women love – and oh! how I loved you. Not Hannah, Samuel more. And you needed love, for you were weakly, and only love could have kept you alive. Only love can keep any one alive. And boys are careless often, and without thinking give pain, and we always fancy that when they come to man's estate and know us better they will repay us. But it is not so. The world draws them from our side, and they make friends with whom they are happier than they are with us, and have amusements from which we are barred, and interests that are not ours; and they are unjust to us often, for when they find life bitter they blame us for it, and when they find it sweet we do not taste its sweetness with them. . . . You made many friends and went into their houses and were glad with them, and I, knowing my secret, did not dare to follow, but stayed at home and closed the door, shut out the sun and sat in darkness. What should I have done in honest households? My past was ever with me. . . . And you thought I didn't care for the pleasant things of life. I tell you I longed for them, but did not dare to touch them, feeling I had no right. You thought I was happier working amongst the poor. That was my mission, you imagined. It was not, but where else was I to go? The sick do not ask if the hand that smooths their pillow is pure, nor the dying care if the lips that touch their brow have known the kiss of sin. It was you I thought of all the time; I gave to them the love you did not need; lavished on them a love that was not theirs. . . . And you thought I spent too much of my time in going to Church, and in Church duties. But where else could I turn? God's house is the only house where sinners are made welcome, and you were always in my heart, Gerald, too much in my heart. For, though day after day, at morn or evensong, I have knelt in God's house, I have never repented of my sin. How could I repent of my sin when you, my love, were its fruit. Even now that you are bitter to me I cannot repent. I do not. You are more to me than innocence. I would rather be your mother – oh! much rather! – than have been always pure. . . . Oh, don't you see? don't you understand? It is my dishonour that has made you so dear to me. It is my disgrace that has bound you so closely to me. It is the price I paid for you – the price of soul and body – that makes me love you as I do. Oh, don't ask me to do this horrible thing. Child of my shame, be still the child of my shame!

Gerald: Mother, I didn't know you loved me so much as that. And I will be a better son to you than I have been. And you and I must never leave each other. . . but, mother. . . I can't help it. . . you must become my father's wife. You must marry him. It is your duty.

Hester (running forward and embracing MRS. ARBUTHNOT): No, no; you shall not. That would be real dishonour, the first you have ever known. That would be real disgrace: the first to touch you. Leave him and come with me. There are other countries than England. . . . Oh! other countries over sea, better, wiser, and less unjust lands. The world is very wide and very big.

Mrs. Arbuthnot: No, not for me. For me the world is shrivelled to a palm's breadth, and where I walk there are thorns.

Hester: It shall not be so. We shall somewhere find green valleys and fresh waters, and if we weep well, we shall weep together. Have we not both loved him?

Gerald: Hester!

Hester (waving him back): Don't, don't! You cannot love me at all unless you love her also. You cannot honour me, unless she's holier to you. In her all womanhood is martyred. Not she alone, but all of us are stricken in her house.

Gerald: Hester, Hester, what shall I do?

Hester: Do you respect the man who is your father?

Gerald: Respect him? I despise him! He is infamous.

Hester: I thank you for saving me from him last night.

Gerald: Ah, that is nothing. I would die to save you. But you don't tell me what to do now!

Hester: Have I not thanked you for saving *me*?

Gerald: But what should I do?

Hester: Ask your own heart, not mine. I never had a mother to save, or shame.

Mrs. Arbuthnot: He is hard – he is hard. Let me go away.

Gerald (rushes over and kneels down beside his mother): Mother, forgive me; I have been to blame.

Mrs. Arbuthnot: Don't kiss my hands; they are cold. My heart is cold; something has broken it.

Hester: Ah, don't say that. Hearts live by being wounded. Pleasure may turn a heart to stone, riches may make it callous, but sorrow – oh, sorrow cannot break it. Besides, what sorrows have you now? Why, at this moment you are more dear to him than ever, *dear* though you have *been*, and oh! how dear you *have* been always. Ah! be kind to him.

Gerald: You are my mother and my father all in one. I need no second parent. It was for you I spoke, for you alone. Oh, say something, mother. Have I but found one love to lose another? Don't tell me that. O mother, you are cruel. *(Gets up and flings himself sobbing on a sofa.)*

Mrs. Arbuthnot (to HESTER*):* But has he found indeed another love?

Hester: You know I have loved him always.

Mrs. Arbuthnot: But we are very poor.

Hester: Who, being loved, is poor? Oh, no one. I hate my riches. They are a burden. Let him share it with me.

Mrs. Arbuthnot: But we are disgraced. We rank among the outcasts. Gerald is nameless. The sins of the parents should be visited on the children. It is God's law.

Hester: I was wrong. God's law is only Love.

Mrs. Arbuthnot (*rises, and taking* HESTER *by the hand goes slowly over to where* GERALD *is lying on the sofa with his head buried in his hands. She touches him and he looks up*): Gerald, I cannot give you a father, but I have brought you a wife.

Gerald: Mother, I am not worthy either of her or you.

Mrs. Arbuthnot: So she comes first, you are worthy. And when you are away, Gerald. . . with. . . her – oh, think of me sometimes. Don't forget me. And when you pray, pray for me. We should pray when we are happiest, and you will be happy, Gerald.

Hester: Oh, you don't think of leaving us?

Gerald: Mother, you won't leave us?

Mrs. Arbuthnot: I might bring shame upon you!

Gerald: Mother!

Mrs. Arbuthnot: For a little then; and if you let me, near you always.

Hester (*to* MRS. ARBUTHNOT): Come out with us to the garden.

Mrs. Arbuthnot: Later on, later on.

Exeunt HESTER *and* GERALD.

MRS. ARBUTHNOT *goes towards door L.C. Stops at looking-glass over mantelpiece and looks into it.*
Enter ALICE *R.C.*

Alice: A gentleman to see you, ma'am.

Mrs. Arbuthnot: Say I am not at home. Show me the card. (*Takes card from salver and looks at it.*) Say I will not see him.

LORD ILLINGWORTH *enters.* MRS. ARBUTHNOT *sees him in the glass and starts, but does not turn round. Exit* ALICE.

What can you have to say to me to-day, George Harford? You can have nothing to say to me. You must leave this house.

Lord Illingworth: Rachel, Gerald knows everything about you and me now, so some arrangement must be come to that will suit us all three. I assure you, he will find in me the most charming and generous of fathers.

Mrs. Arbuthnot: My son may come in at any moment. I saved you last night. I may not be able to save you again. My son feels my dishonour strongly, terribly strongly. I beg you to go.

Lord Illingworth (*sitting down*): Last night was excessively unfortunate. That silly Puritan girl making a scene merely because I wanted to kiss her. What harm is there in a kiss?

Mrs. Arbuthnot (*turning round*): A kiss may ruin a human life, George Harford. I know that. I know that too well.

Lord Illingworth: We won't discuss that at present. What is of importance to-day, as yesterday, is still our son. I am extremely fond of him, as you know, and odd though it may seem to you, I admired his conduct last night immensely. He took up the cudgels for that pretty prude with wonderful promptitude. He is just what I should have liked a son of mine to be. Except that no son of mine should ever take the side of the Puritans; that is always an error. Now, what I propose is this.

Mrs. Arbuthnot: Lord Illingworth, no proposition of yours interests me.

Lord Illingworth: According to our ridiculous English laws, I can't legitimise Gerald. But I can leave him my property. Illingworth is entailed, of course, but it is a tedious barrack of a place. He can have Ashby, which is much prettier, Harborough, which has the best shooting in the north of England, and the house in St. James's Square. What more can a gentleman desire in this world?

Mrs. Arbuthnot: Nothing more, I am quite sure.

Lord Illingworth: As for a title, a title is really rather a nuisance in these democratic days. As George Harford I had everything I wanted. Now I have merely everything that other people want, which isn't nearly so pleasant. Well, my proposal is this.

Mrs. Arbuthnot: I told you I was not interested, and I beg you to go.

Lord Illingworth: The boy is to be with you for six months in the year, and with me for the other six. That is perfectly fair, is it not? You can have whatever allowance you like, and live where you choose. As for your past, no one knows anything about it except myself and Gerald. There is the Puritan, of course, the Puritan in white muslin, but she doesn't count. She couldn't tell the story without explaining that she objected to being kissed, could she? And all the women would think her a fool and the men think her a bore. And you need not be afraid that Gerald won't be my heir. I needn't tell you I have not the slightest intention of marrying.

Mrs. Arbuthnot: You come too late. My son has no need of you. You are not necessary.

Lord Illingworth: What do you mean, Rachel?

Mrs. Arbuthnot: That you are not necessary to Gerald's career. He does not require you.

Lord Illingworth: I do not understand you.

Mrs. Arbuthnot: Look into the garden. (LORD ILLING-WORTH *rises and goes towards window.*) You had better not let them see you; you bring unpleasant memories. (LORD ILLING-WORTH *looks out and starts.*) She loves him. They love each other. We are safe from you, and we are going away.

Lord Illingworth: Where?

Mrs. Arbuthnot: We will not tell you, and if you find us we will not know you. You seem surprised. What welcome would you get from the girl whose lips you tried to soil, from the boy whose life you have shamed, from the mother whose dishonour comes from you?

Lord Illingworth: You have grown hard, Rachel.

Mrs. Arbuthnot: I was too weak once. It is well for me that I have changed.

Lord Illingworth: I was very young at the time. We men know life too early.

Mrs. Arbuthnot: And we women know life too late. That is the difference between men and women. (*A pause.*)

Lord Illingworth: Rachel, I want my son. My money may be of no use to him now. I may be of no use to him, but I want my son. Bring us together, Rachel. You can do it if you choose. (*Sees letter on table.*)

Mrs. Arbuthnot: There is no room in my boy's life for you. He is not interested in you.

Lord Illingworth: Then why does he write to me?

Mrs. Arbuthnot: What do you mean?

Lord Illingworth: What letter is this? (*Takes up letter.*)

Mrs. Arbuthnot: That – is nothing. Give it to me.

Lord Illingworth: It is addressed to me.

Mrs. Arbuthnot: You are not to open it. I forbid you to open it.

Lord Illingworth: And in Gerald's handwriting.

Mrs. Arbuthnot: It was not to have been sent. It is a letter he wrote to you this morning, before he saw me. But he is sorry now he wrote it, very sorry. You are not to open it. Give it to me.

Lord Illingworth: It belongs to me. (*Opens it, sits down and reads it slowly.* MRS. ARBUTHNOT *watches him all the time.*) You have read this letter, I suppose, Rachel?

Mrs. Arbuthnot: No.

Lord Illingworth: You know what is in it?

Mrs. Arbuthnot: Yes!

Lord Illingworth: I don't admit for a moment that the boy is right in what he says. I don't admit that it is any duty of mine to marry you. I deny it entirely. But to get my son back I am ready – yes, I am ready to marry you, Rachel – and to treat you always with the deference and respect due to my wife. I will marry you as soon as you choose. I give you my word of honour.

Mrs. Arbuthnot: You made that promise to me once before and broke it.

Lord Illingworth: I will keep it now. And that will show you that I love my son, at least as much as you love him. For when I marry you, Rachel, there are some ambitions I shall have to surrender. High ambitions, too, if any ambition is high.

Mrs. Arbuthnot: I decline to marry you, Lord Illingworth.

Lord Illingworth: Are you serious?

Mrs. Arbuthnot: Yes.

Lord Illingworth: Do tell me your reasons. They would interest me enormously.

Mrs. Arbuthnot: I have already explained them to my son.

Lord Illingworth: I suppose they were intensely sentimental, weren't they? You women live by your emotions and for them. You have no philosophy of life.

Mrs. Arbuthnot: You are right. We women live by our emotions and for them. By our passions, and for them, if you will. I have two passions, Lord Illngworth: my love of him, my hate of you. You cannot kill those. They feed each other.

Lord Illingworth: What sort of love is that which needs to have hate as its brother?

Mrs. Arbuthnot: It is the sort of love I have for Gerald. Do you think that terrible? Well, it is terrible. All love is terrible. All love is a tragedy. I loved you once, Lord Illingworth. Oh, what a tragedy for a woman to have loved you!

Lord Illingworth: So you really refuse to marry me?

Mrs. Arbuthnot: Yes.

Lord Illingworth: Because you hate me?

Mrs. Arbuthnot: Yes.

Lord Illingworth: And does my son hate me as you do?

Mrs. Arbuthnot: No.

Lord Illingworth: I am glad of that, Rachel.

Mrs. Arbuthnot: He merely despises you.

Lord Illingworth: What a pity! What a pity for him, I mean.

Mrs. Arbuthnot: Don't be deceived, George. Children begin by loving their parents. After a time they judge them. Rarely if ever do they forgive them.

Lord Illingworth (reads letter over again, very slowly): May I ask by what arguments you made the boy who wrote this letter, this beautiful, passionate letter, believe that you should not marry his father, the father of your own chid?

Mrs. Arbuthnot: It was not I who made him see it. It was another.

Lord Illingworth: What *fin-de-siècle* person?

Mrs. Arbuthnot: The Puritan, Lord Illingworth. (*A pause.*)

Lord Illingworth (winces, then rises slowly and goes over to table where his hat and gloves are. MRS. ARBUTHNOT is standing close to the table. He picks up one of the gloves, and begins putting it on): There is not much then for me to do here, Rachel?

Mrs. Arbuthnot: Nothing.

Lord Illingworth: It is good-bye, is it?

Mrs. Arbuthnot: For ever, I hope, this time, Lord Illingworth.

Lord Illingworth: How curious! At this moment you look exactly as you looked the night you left me twenty years ago. You have just the same expression in your mouth. Upon my word, Rachel, no woman ever loved me as you did. Why, you gave yourself to me like a flower, to do anything I liked with. You were the prettiest of playthings, the most fascinating of small romances. . . (*Pulls out watch.*) Quarter to two! Must be strolling back to Hunstanton. Don't suppose I shall see you there again. I'm sorry, I am, really. It's been an amusing experience to have met amongst people of one's own rank, and treated quite seriously too, one's mistress and one's –

MRS. ARBUTHNOT *snatches up glove and strikes* LORD ILLINGWORTH *across the face with it.* LORD ILLINGWORTH *starts. He is dazed by the insult of his punishment. Then he controls himself and goes to window and looks out at his son. Sighs and leaves the room.*

Mrs. Arbuthnot (falls sobbing on the sofa): He would have said it. He would have said it.

Enter GERALD *and* HESTER *from the garden.*

Gerald: Well, dear mother. You never came out after all. So we have come in to fetch you. Mother, you have not been crying? (*Kneels down beside her.*)

Mrs. Arbuthnot: My boy! My boy! My boy! (*Running her fingers through his hair.*)

Hester (*coming over*): But you have two children now. You'll let me be your daughter?

Mrs. Arbuthnot (*looking up*): Would you choose me for a mother?

Hester: You of all women I have ever known.

They move towards the door leading into garden with their arms round each other's waists. GERALD goes to table L.C. for his hat. On turning round he sees LORD ILLINGWORTH'S glove lying on the floor, and picks it up.

Gerald: Hallo, mother, whose glove is this? You have had a visitor. Who was it?

Mrs. Arbuthnot (*turning round*): Oh! no one. No one in particular. A man of no importance.

CURTAIN.

WORDSWORTH CLASSICS

General Editors: Marcus Clapham & Clive Reynard

JANE AUSTEN
Emma
Mansfield Park
Northanger Abbey
Persuasion
Pride and Prejudice
Sense and Sensibility

ARNOLD BENNETT
Anna of the Five Towns

R. D. BLACKMORE
Lorna Doone

ANNE BRONTË
Agnes Grey
*The Tenant of
Wildfell Hall*

CHARLOTTE BRONTË
Jane Eyre
The Professor
Shirley
Villette

EMILY BRONTË
Wuthering Heights

JOHN BUCHAN
Greenmantle
Mr Standfast
The Thirty-Nine Steps

SAMUEL BUTLER
The Way of All Flesh

LEWIS CARROLL
Alice in Wonderland

CERVANTES
Don Quixote

G. K. CHESTERTON
*Father Brown:
Selected Stories*
*The Man who was
Thursday*

ERSKINE CHILDERS
The Riddle of the Sands

JOHN CLELAND
*Memoirs of a Woman of
Pleasure: Fanny Hill*

WILKIE COLLINS
The Moonstone
The Woman in White

JOSEPH CONRAD
Heart of Darkness
Lord Jim
The Secret Agent

J. FENIMORE COOPER
*The Last of the
Mohicans*

STEPHEN CRANE
*The Red Badge of
Courage*

THOMAS DE QUINCEY
*Confessions of an English
Opium Eater*

DANIEL DEFOE
Moll Flanders
Robinson Crusoe

CHARLES DICKENS
Bleak House
David Copperfield
Great Expectations
Hard Times
Little Dorrit
Martin Chuzzlewit
Oliver Twist
Pickwick Papers
A Tale of Two Cities

BENJAMIN DISRAELI
Sybil

THEODOR DOSTOEVSKY
Crime and Punishment

**SIR ARTHUR CONAN
DOYLE**
*The Adventures of
Sherlock Holmes*
*The Case-Book of
Sherlock Holmes*
*The Lost World &
Other Stories*
*The Return of
Sherlock Holmes*
Sir Nigel

GEORGE DU MAURIER
Trilby

ALEXANDRE DUMAS
The Three Musketeers

MARIA EDGEWORTH
Castle Rackrent

GEORGE ELIOT
The Mill on the Floss
Middlemarch
Silas Marner

HENRY FIELDING
Tom Jones

F. SCOTT FITZGERALD
*A Diamond as Big as the
Ritz & Other Stories*
The Great Gatsby
Tender is the Night

GUSTAVE FLAUBERT
Madame Bovary

JOHN GALSWORTHY
In Chancery
The Man of Property
To Let

ELIZABETH GASKELL
Cranford
North and South

KENNETH GRAHAME
*The Wind in the
Willows*

**GEORGE & WEEDON
GROSSMITH**
Diary of a Nobody

RIDER HAGGARD
She

THOMAS HARDY
*Far from the
Madding Crowd*
The Mayor of Casterbridge
*The Return of the
Native*
Tess of the d'Urbervilles
The Trumpet Major
*Under the Greenwood
Tree*

DISTRIBUTION

AUSTRALIA & PAPUA NEW GUINEA
Peribo Pty Ltd
58 Beaumont Road, Mount Kuring-Gai
NSW 2080, Australia
Tel: (02) 457 0011 Fax: (02) 457 0022

CZECH REPUBLIC
Bohemian Ventures s r. o.,
Delnicka 13, 170 00 Prague 7
Tel: 042 2 877837 Fax: 042 2 801498

FRANCE
Copernicus Diffusion
23 Rue Saint Dominique, Paris 75007
Tel: 1 44 11 33 20 Fax: 1 44 11 33 21

GERMANY & AUSTRIA
**GLBmbH (Bargain, Promotional
& Remainder Shops)**
Zollstockgürtel 5, 50969 Köln
Tel: 0221 34 20 92 Fax: 0221 38 40 40

**Tradis Verlag und Vertrieb GmbH
(Bookshops)**
Postfach 90 03 69, D-51113 Köln
Tel: 022 03 31059 Fax: 022 03 3 93 40

GREAT BRITAIN & IRELAND
Wordsworth Editions Ltd
Cumberland House, Crib Street
Ware, Hertfordshire SG12 9ET

INDIA
OM Book Service
1690 First Floor, Nai Sarak, Delhi – 110006
Tel: 3279823-3265303 Fax: 3278091

ISRAEL
Timmy Marketing Limited
Israel Ben Zeev 12, Ramont Gimmel, Jerusalem
Tel: 02-865266 Fax: 02-880035

ITALY
Magis Books s.p.a.
Via Raffaello 31/C, Zona Ind Mancasale
42100 Reggio Emilia
Tel: 0522 920999 Fax: 0522 920666

NEW ZEALAND & FIJI
Allphy Book Distributors Ltd
4-6 Charles Street, Eden Terrace, Auckland,
Tel: (09) 3773096 Fax: (09) 3022770

MALAYSIA & BRUNEI
Vintrade SDN BHD
5 & 7 Lorong Datuk Sulaiman 7
Taman Tun Dr Ismail
60000 Kuala Lumpur, Malaysia
Tel: (603) 717 3333 Fax: (603) 719 2942

MALTA & GOZO
Agius & Agius Ltd
42A South Street, Valletta VLT 11
Tel: 234038 - 220347 Fax: 241175

NORTH AMERICA
Universal Sales & Marketing
230 Fifth Avenue, Suite 1212
New York, NY 10001, USA
Tel: 212 481 3500 Fax: 212 481 3534

PHILIPPINES
I J Sagun Enterprises
P O Box 4322 CPO Manila
2 Topaz Road, Greenheights Village,
Taytay, Rizal
Tel: 631 80 61 TO 66

PORTUGAL
International Publishing Services Ltd
Rua da Cruz da Carreira, 4B, 1100 Lisbon
Tel: 01 570051 Fax: 01 3522066

SOUTHERN & CENTRAL AFRICA
Southern Book Publishers (Pty) Ltd
P.O.Box 3103
Halfway House 1685, South Africa
Tel: (011) 315-3633/4/5/6
Fax: (011) 315-3810

EAST AFRICA & KENYA
P.M.C. International Importers & Exporters CC
Unit 6, Ben-Sarah Place, 52-56 Columbine Place,
Glen Anil, Kwa-Zulu Natal 4051,
P.O.Box 201520,
Durban North, Kwa-Zulu Natal 4016
Tel: (031) 844441 Fax: (031) 844466

SINGAPORE
Paul & Elizabeth Book Services Pte Ltd
163 Tanglin Road No 03-15/16
Tanglin Mall, Singapore 1024
Tel: (65) 735 7308 Fax: (65) 735 9747

SLOVAK REPUBLIC
Slovak Ventures s r. o.,
Stefanikova 128, 949 01 Nitra
Tel/Fax: 042 87 525105/6/7

SPAIN
Ribera Libros, S.L.
Poligono Martiartu, Calle 1 - no 6
48480 Arrigorriaga, Vizcaya
Tel: 34 4 6713607 (Almacen)
     34 4 4418787 (Libreria)
Fax: 34 4 6713608 (Almacen)
     34 4 4418029 (Libreria)

UNITED ARAB EMIRATES
Nadoo Trading LLC
P.O.Box 3186
Dubai
United Arab Emirates
Tel: 04-359793 Fax: 04-487157

DIRECT MAIL **Bibliophile Books**
5 Thomas Road, London E14 7BN,
Tel: 0171-515 9222 Fax: 0171-538 4115
Order hotline 24 hours Tel: 0171-515 9555
Cash with order + £2.00 p&p (UK)